First Edition

Copyright © 2021 Christopher D. Wayland

All rights reserved. No part of this book may be reproduced or transmitted in any form or by any means, electronic or mechanical, including photocopying, recording or by any information storage and retrieval system without written permission from the publisher.

BROOKLYNNE WORKS – Madison, Wisconsin ISBN: 978-0-578-82415-4
Library of Congress Control Number: pending Title: *Elspeth*
Author: Christopher D. Wayland
Digital distribution | 2021
Paperback | 2021

This novel is a work of fiction. The characters, names, incidents, places, and dialogue are products of the author's imagination, and are not to be construed as real.

Cover design by Junior McLean @ Junior's Digital Designs

P.O. Box 258136
Madison, WI 53725

Also by Christopher D. Wayland
From Brooklynne Works, available online through fine retailers everywhere

Crossing the Meadow (2019)

Chip McArcher, about to head into the fifth grade, is having a difficult summer. He's suffered the loss of a beloved pet. His father is away from home on business most of the time. And two local bullies have cornered him into meeting a frightening challenge: he must cross the neighborhood meadow after dark, alone, without the aid of a flashlight, or suffer humiliation at the start of the next school year.

"When I read <u>Crossing the Meadow</u>, it gave me an amazing feeling. The first paragraph caught my full attention. My two favorite series of books were outdone by this amazing story. In every part I thought to myself, WHAT'S GOING TO HAPPEN NEXT!!! I love this book!"
- Evelyn Simons, fourth-grader

Elspeth

Christopher D. Wayland

"An intriguing story. I think both kids and adults will enjoy it. I don't want to give away the ending, but [Chip's night walk] is rather harrowing."

- George Smith, Bangor Daily News

"Beautifully written with evocative passages, <u>Crossing the Meadow</u> isn't at all what I expected. I'd have to say the meadow plays just as important a character as the human beings in this book. Highly recommended."

- Rod Labbe, author of <u>The Blue Classroom</u>

"At 59 pages, this is a short read, but I am amazed at the emotional impact it has. Wayland creates a number of truly three-dimensional characters. Some of the paramount fears of growing up, such as grief, mortality, bullying and uncertainty in the company of peers, are superbly addressed. Things come to a suspenseful climax in the titular meadow. Wonderful storytelling."

- Eric Dodson

"<u>Crossing the Meadow</u> is a fine book. It is easy to read and does not talk down to the reader. Exceptionally good is the way [Mr. Wayland] draws the reader into the imagination of Chip, building carefully and well to the astonishing conclusion."

- Samuel C. Brown, Jr.

Dedication

The publication of this book was made possible by
the generous support of

Marshall and Jacquie Elzinga
Kay Landry
Alice and Jon Olson
Laura Kee
Bruce Habowski
Asbel Rivera
Sam, Jr. And Baya Brown
Philip Forman
John E. Sparks
Susan Brown

Many extra thanks for those who contributed to the editing and fine-tuning of the book (it takes a neighborhood to raise a manuscript!):

Alice Olson, (a selflessly dedicated proof-reader)
John Sidelinger
Jeremy Ferguson
Mary Habowski
Kay Landry
Erica M. Hughes

CONTENTS

Chapter 1 *Nikki and Elspeth Walk Home as Usual, But* 1
Chapter 2 *Damon Joins the Girls For Lunch* 5
Chapter 3 *Grammar* 9
Chapter 4 *Best Friends in Crisis* 13
Chapter 5 *Where Is Damon?* 20
Chapter 6 *Over Night Mare* 25
Chapter 7 *Saturday* 34
Chapter 8 *A Few Good Moments* 38
Chapter 9 *The Big Day Before the Big Night* 42
Chapter 10 *Memento Mori* 49
Chapter 11 *Into the House* 57
Chapter 12 *Everything Changed* 69
Chapter 13 *...But Some Things Changed Back* 74
Chapter 14 *The Air Was Thick On Friday* 80
Chapter 15 *The Card* 84
Chapter 16 *Peccadillos* 89
Chapter 17 *Process* 93
Chapter 18 *Visitor* 99
Chapter 19 *The Same Much* 105
Chapter 20 *Bonding with Patrick, And Again With Nikki* 110
Chapter 21 *No More Visitors Wanted* 114
Chapter 22 *It's All in the Wrist* 121
Chapter 23 *In Memoriam* 128
Chapter 24 *Daddy Time* 133
Chapter 25 *The Camp Out, Part One – Patrick's Revelation* 140
Chapter 26 *The Camp Out, Part Two – No*

Mosquitos, But 145
Chapter 27 *Learning a Little More* 153
Chapter 28 *Finding Hope In a Newfound Friend* .
....158
Chapter 29 *The House on Bax and Beechum*
   Streets 164
Chapter 30 *The Old Lady, and the Way Back To*
   Normal 178
Chapter 31 *Theories* 185
Chapter 32 *Coda* 188

For Evelyn

Chapter 1
Nikki and Elspeth Walk Home as Usual, But...

On the corner of Bax and Beechum streets there lives a house.

Or, at least, it is certainly alive for all the neighborhood children. For thirty-seven years, no one has occupied it. No one you can *see*, that is.

The outside walls are shedding their pale yellow paint. Its roof is buckling and has thrown off dozens of moss-covered shingles like a dog shaking water from its fur. The high, square posts supporting the overhang above the front entrance look bowed and fatigued. Vandals throwing rocks and bottles through its filmy windows have left nary an unbroken pane.

There isn't a right angle anywhere now. The entire structure leans a bit to one side, as if in its death throes, but never quite falling in. What once had been a lawn is now an unkempt, overgrown tangle of lifeless grass and twisted weeds. The mailbox at the street end of the long-neglected walkway is missing, its post now leaning like the mast of a sinking ship. It's the kind of place you'd think of first when you wanted to conjure a haunted house in your head.

There are neighborhoods everywhere still inhabited by a single dilapidated house that people no longer live in but which no one has the heart or the legal right to bulldoze into memory. Neighbors living on both Bax and Beechum Streets complain– and will no doubt continue to complain – about this eyesore on the corner, while others champion its restoration, as it is the only remaining Victorian structure in Siteson.

In any case, for the time being, it serves as both a nightmare and a delight for every kid who lives along the streets nearby. As long as it remains standing, it provides them with endless fodder for boasting and dares and stories of wild imagining.

But the sound of a shrill baying from within its walls one Tuesday afternoon not long ago certainly *wasn't* any wild imagining. Not for Elspeth and her best-and-almost-only friend Nikki.

Elspeth, who was ten, did not hang out with a regular gaggle of classmates, who mostly ignored her because, well, she *must* be a snob, raising her hand in class for nearly every question the teacher asked. And they brushed her off because she wasn't much into sports. And they whispered behind her back and giggled because she had a prosthetic right leg just below the knee. But she had a cheery smile that ended in a dimple on only one side of her face, which was faintly speckled with freckles one could only see when standing close to her.

Nikki Pettengill treated her like just plain Elspeth Amesbury, fourth grader, because Elspeth was her best-and-almost-only friend, too. Taller than Elspeth, with dark hair and eyes, Nikki had a husky-ish voice and was easily agitated. They made a good pair, never running out of things to talk about.

Their walks back from school – eleven blocks for Nikki and two further along for Elspeth – took them past the old yellow house, which had never been a problem in the past. On this particular October day, as dusk was quickly approaching, the two friends had stayed late at school for the occasional crafts workshop, where they'd made pumpkin sculptures from papier-mâché.

Nikki was happily walk-skipping along, thinking about Halloween, getting a bit ahead of Elspeth, who could not skip. The girls maneuvered the sidewalk between blowing leaves they pretended were bombs that would explode if touched. They had just turned the corner onto Beechum Street where they both lived, talking about very personal stuff, as best friends often do.

Nikki stopped short and grabbed Elspeth's arm. "Wait. Listen!"

At first, all Elspeth could hear was the crispy fluttering of dry leaves that remained on the trees and those bouncing along the cement blocks of the sidewalk. But then, faintly, she discerned something that clearly wasn't the breeze or the leaves. It was a direful moaning, like that of a wounded animal, and it seemed to be emerging from inside the decaying house now before them. "What the...?"

"Shh!" Nikki said, holding her finger to her mouth. It was still warm enough for wearing short-sleeves, and Elspeth noticed goosebumps rising on her still-tanned arms. But the strange sound soon faded into the ambiance of traffic and wind and whatever else comprised the everyday noise of this street, in this neighborhood, in this town of Siteson at five-fifteen in the darkening late-autumn afternoon.

Elspeth said, "That was a dog. I think."

"Yeah," Nikki whispered.

"But, why is there a dog in that house? How did it get in?"

"It's probably a stray, and found an open door or something."

"Well then, someone ought to take care of it. But that crying sounded so *eerie*. Maybe it's a..." Elspeth stopped, and shook her head. "Nah."

"What? Maybe it's a *what*?"

"Maybe it's not a real *live* dog."

"Oh, come on, 'Speth! Are you saying that it might be a spirit dog or something? Why would you think that?" Elspeth shrugged her shoulders. "You have really weird thoughts sometimes."

The girls stood in place, staring at the house as the reddish-gray clouds slowly descended overhead, and shadows lengthened until they vanished completely.

"I gotta get home," Nikki said, and they hastily walked to their respective driveways.

On that day, the girls came to suspect that something might be living in the house on the corner of Bax and Beechum streets, after all these years.

Chapter 2
Damon Joins the Girls for Lunch

October 31 was just around the corner and, of course, most every kid in the country was ramped up and making plans for costumes and parties and trick-or-treating. School teachers were facing classrooms full of distracted pupils who weren't learning much except about what their friends were going to do on the Big Night.

Elspeth was planning on trick-or-treating with Nikki, and maybe with their sometimes friend Damon Clarke, who occasionally joined them at their school lunch table, but who generally hung out with some of the boys. He was well-enough liked by most fourth graders that no one hassled him much, no matter who he spent time with.

On this day, October 24, exactly one week before Halloween, Damon sat down beside Nikki and across from Elspeth, his lunch tray in front of him. His ruffled hair, amber-brown eyes and slightly pointed ears gave him an impish look. "I don't know about you," he said, "but I'm sick of fish sticks and tater tots. I'm bringing my own lunch from now on."

Nikki piped in. "Hey, if you don't want your taters, hand 'em over!"

"Want the fish sticks, too? And the green beans?"

"Nah. You can keep those. Besides, you gotta eat

*some*thing."

"Well, that's what the chocolate chip cookie's for."

Elspeth asked him, "So, are you going to go trick-or-treating with us?"

"Dunno. Haven't decided. I might go with Patrick and Nate. Depends."

"On what?" Elspeth asked.

"On who they're going as. If they want to go as superheroes, I'll go with you guys. I can't stand Superman and Batman and all those dudes." Nikki clammed up. She'd been planning to go as Wonder Woman.

The lunchroom with its glazed, green tile walls was filled with the smell of beans and fish and sweaty kids who were fresh out of gym class. All along the walls on tables were the paper pumpkins the kids had made after school the day before. Very few kids were bothering to look at them. This was, after all, a lunchroom, not a museum.

The two teachers who were on lunch duty stood like police detectives on either side of the room, checking to make sure no food got wasted and no one was throwing tater tots across the room. "They never give us enough time to eat," Nikki complained. "We're always the last in line just because our classroom is the farthest from the cafeteria, and we only have about fifteen minutes. That's not fair. And I forgot to get ketchup!"

"Here," Damon said, tossing a couple of packets to her. "You can have mine."

"The principal's trying to talk us into going to a school party instead of trick-or-treating. Does anyone actually go to those?" Elspeth asked.

"Yeah, I know a few kids who do," Damon said, swigging a mouthful of milk from his cardboard container. "Why anyone would want to come here at night after they had to be here all day long is a mystery to me. And even the kids who go trick-or-treating...a lot of them have to be driven around by their parents. That's no fun."

"Can someone open this for me?" Elspeth asked. "Sorry. Sometimes I can't get them open right and I wind up spilling milk everywhere."

"Give it here," Damon said, squeezing the top of her milk carton, which opened like a paper fortune teller. "Jeez, Elspeth, you'd flunk if we got grades for that."

Fourth graders were already carrying their trays to the window and starting to form lines to leave the lunch room.

Elspeth and Nikki felt suddenly rushed and began wolfing down their food, while Damon squeezed his empty milk carton wide open and spooned his beans and fish into it before closing it back up.

Pointing to the gold-colored ring on Damon's forefinger, Nikki said, "That's really nice."

"Look...my initials are engraved in it, see? 'D.C.' for Damon Clarke. My grammy gave it to me. She died last year. It ain't real gold, but who cares? She couldn't afford real gold anyway."

"Looks good on you," Nikki said. Then she added: "Hey, we heard a dog howling from the old house yesterday. We couldn't see it, but we could hear it. Right, 'Speth?"

"Um-hum," her friend confirmed, while chewing. "It was definitely from inside the house. I think."

"Well, why don't you go check it out?"

Nikki said, "Oh, no! No *way* am I going in there!"

Damon said, "Anyway, I'll let you know tomorrow if I'm going with you on Halloween. But my class is lining up, so I'll see ya." He carried his tray with one hand and shuffled toward the front of the room, emptying it into the trash as one of the lunch room proctors looked on.

"I hope he goes with us Tuesday night. It would feel a little, I dunno..."

"Safer?" Nikki asked.

"Um, yeah. He's a boy and all."

"What difference does *that* make? I mean, right?"

"I know. But, well, it would just be nice if he came along."

Nikki put on a squinty, accusatory face. "You got a thing for him, don'tcha?"

"Don't be an idiot. No, I don't have 'a thing' for him. C'mon, we need to get in line."

"You have tartar sauce on your mouth."

"Oh," Elspeth said, wiping it off with her shirt sleeve. "Thanks. Talk to you after school."

And with that, another in an endless string of hurried school lunches came to an end.

But Elspeth had much to preoccupy her during the afternoon, even as her teacher demonstrated how to diagram a sentence. There was Halloween night. And Damon. And the dog in the house on the corner of Bax and Beechum Streets.

Chapter 3
Grammar

Rewrite this sentence with corrections:
oh my oh me cried mrs mcgee i think i'll climb that apple tree
  Due on Thursday.

That was one of Elspeth's grammar homework questions on Wednesday, and she spent over a half hour on it before giving up in defeat. She was usually great with English, but this sentence was tricky.

She walked downstairs to the kitchen, where her mother was stirring sauce for spaghetti. "Mom? Can you help me with this?"

"With what, sweetie?"

"I got a question."

"You *have* a question."

"Yeah, I *have* a question, about my homework assignment."

"Well, you know the agreement between you and me and your dad, which is that you have to finish it the best way you can, and then we'll look at it and make suggestions. But *you* have to do the work."

"I know, but I *have* done it the best way I can. It's just all these damn...sorry...all these dumb commas and apostrophes and quotation marks I have to put in the right places."

"Read it to me."

Elspeth read the sentence needing punctuation and capital letters. "I got some of it, but I don't know if it's right. Could you check it, please?" Her mother was sipping the sauce from a wooden spoon and making a face that suggested it was good, but needed a bit more seasoning. "Mom?"

"Yes, dear, I heard you. Who will you be trick-or-treating with next week?"

The question took Elspeth completely out of her concern about homework. "Well, Nikki, of course."

"Of course."

"And maybe Damon."

"Damon? Do I know Damon?"

"He's a kid from school." The kitchen was smelling strongly of oregano and making Elspeth's mouth fill with hunger saliva. "When's dinner?"

"Come on now, you know your father gets home at about six. But that's not for a half-hour, so go tackle that homework some more. Then I'll look at it."

Having brought the assignment back up to her room, she spent another twenty-five minutes adding this and crossing out that and moving quotation marks all over the sentence. Finally, she decided maybe she would just turn it in as it was.

As always, she jumped up into her father's arms the moment he came through the door. She kissed his cheek, loosened his tie, and unbuttoned his collar while he held her, before she slipped down to the floor. He seemed a bit tense, but that wasn't unusual after a day at the real estate office. "Are you okay, Daddy?"

"I'm fine, Little Squirrel. How about you? Good

day in school?"

"Nothing much happened. Fish sticks for lunch."

"Mmm, yummy!" Dad said.

"Ew, yucky!" Elspeth said, and they both laughed.

Her dad hugged and kissed her mom, which always made Elspeth feel happy and protected. They'd been through some rough times since the accident, arguing a lot and scaring Elspeth, who worried they would break up and leave her with just one parent at home. She often thought it was her fault, and that kept her awake many nights. But lately, Mom and Dad seemed to be pretty grounded. Apparently everything was fine, for the moment. She'd take what she could get.

She imagined that Damon's parents were not at all like hers, because Damon had once told her and Nikki that his dad had come home drunk one night and thrown a glass against the living room wall, right over his mother's head. Damon had to hide his little brother under his bed until his father was asleep.

"Dinner will be ready as soon as I've tossed the salad," Mom said.

"I'll toss it for you!" Elspeth volunteered, with a mischievous grin. "I'll toss it all over the kitchen!"

"Okay, silly, why don't you pour milk for yourself and water for us, okay? And feed Lucie while you're at it."

"No problem!" Elspeth poured the drinks, and some milk into Lucie's tiny cat bowl in the corner. She helped Mom dry the dishes after dinner, and then strode into the living room carrying her homework assignment. "Daddy? Could you look at this and see if I did it right?"

"What is it?" he asked from his favorite armchair,

while the television news droned quietly away.

"It's a sentence I'm supposed to punctuate. I don't know if I got it right."

"Sure," Dad said. "Hop on up." Elspeth climbed onto her father's lap holding a piece of lined paper.

"Wow. That *is* a bit of a challenge, isn't it? Looks pretty good, though...except I think there needs to be a comma after 'me,' and then end quotes. Do you see why?"

"Um, because Mrs. McGee stopped talking for a minute?"

"Exactly. And I think that will do it."

"Thanks, Daddy. Daddy, you know that old house on the corner on the way to school?"

"Sure, I know it well."

"Did you ever hear anything weird from in there?"

"Like what?"

"Like, maybe a dog howling or something."

"No, it hasn't been occupied since..."

"We heard one today. Nikki and I."

"A dog? You sure it was from *inside* the house?"

"Positive. Well, *almost* positive."

"I lived on Sizemore Street until I was in high school, even closer to your school than where we live now. We used to walk by that old house all the time. It was empty even back then. I suppose a dog could hide out in there. But, hey, Little Squirrel, it's time to wrap up your day and hop into bed."

"Okay, Daddy."

Dad and Mom tucked Elspeth in and left her bedroom door a tiny bit ajar for the cat to get through. She felt cozy and safe, and fell easily to sleep.

Chapter 4
Best Friends in Crisis

There was something sad in the gray morning air as Elspeth told her mom goodbye, stepped off her doorstep, and walked to the curb to await the school bus. She couldn't figure out why she felt so strange and empty inside. With Halloween only six days off, and confident that her homework was done correctly, there didn't seem to be any particular reason for her to feel like this.

Today her mom had set out her favorite pair of jeans that were a bit frayed at the hems, and a bright red pullover shirt. She'd wanted for years to wear a dress and leggings, like she had when she was six, but her prosthesis was uneven and would make the stockings look lumpy in some places. Her sneakers were the black ankle ones with the big blue stars, which she wore nearly every day. Her yellow, shoulder-length hair was pulled back and held in place with two red barrettes. She looked casual but fashionable, and felt comfortable on this 70-degree day, but just couldn't shake her strange mood and felt completely dispirited.

"Oh my, oh me," cried Mrs. Magee, "I think I'll climb that apple tree!" she murmured, picturing the fully-punctuated sentence in her mind.

Yes, she'd done it correctly. Probably. Maybe she

didn't need a comma between "Oh my" and "oh me." Anyway, that's the way she was going to turn in the assignment.

She was feeling bad for Damon. Could that be it? Nice boy. He didn't always have a very clean neck, and his orange hair was usually not combed very neatly. And his clothes were mostly poorly matched and ruffled. But, he was polite to her and to Nikki, and Elspeth liked him. She wished he would join them for lunch more often, but she understood that he needed to keep up appearances with the boys, too.

Damon lived on the other side of the school from her, where the houses were smaller and the lawns were narrower, and where scruffy dogs without leashes always seemed to be knocking over garbage cans, leaving piles of rubbish which the neighborhood cats and racoons would further scatter about. She had never walked that far along Bax Street, even with Nikki, although Damon had invited them to come over after school a few times while his dad was at work. Nor could she convince Damon to visit her on Beechum Street. He said that his father wouldn't let him go there because it was too far away, and if he did go, he'd be punished. So, they met only at school sometimes, during lunch or recess.

So, maybe thinking of Damon's home life was what made her so gloomy.

But, no, she decided that wasn't really why. She figured that perhaps it was the dog...the dog that had whined from the old house a few days before. Elspeth loved all animals, and the thought that there might be a lonely, abandoned dog there made her think Damon could be right – she should sneak into the house to see if one was living there.

The bus pulled alongside the curb and the driver left her seat, offering as always to help her up the steps, but Elspeth wanted to do it herself. She handed over her backpack full of books, and pulled herself up the three steep steps, using the handrail. A few kids could always be heard quietly mumbling because it took her so long.

Inside the bus that morning, there was the smell of popcorn from somebody's bag lunch and also of shampoo, an odd combination which made her a little queasy. And the diesel fumes from the bus exhaust would only make it worse. There was low chattering and occasional laughter buzzing among most of the thirty-six seats, except for one voice that was louder and was aimed at Elspeth as she passed by. "Here comes Peg-leg!" Some of the other kids sniggered. This happened nearly every day.

Outwardly, she ignored the remark, but in her heart she was desperately close to crying. Making her way to her usual seat near the back, she side-stepped in front of Nikki and sat beside her. The girls swapped places every day to give each a chance at the window.

They sat silently for several minutes before Nikki said, "Hey, are you okay?"

"Yeah," Elspeth said, while her eyes locked on to the old house as they passed it.

"You've been thinking about that place, haven't you?"

"A lot. Seems different to me now than it used to."

"That's because you're worried about that dog."

"Yeah," Elspeth agreed. All at once, she buried her face in her hands and began to sob.

"Hey, 'Speth..." Nikki whispered, putting her right arm around her friend's shoulder. "Don't let what that idiot says to you about your leg..."

"No, it isn't that." But really, it *was* that, on top of the sadness she'd already felt before boarding the bus.

Nikki leaned across her friend, pulled in the side tabs, and pushed their window up. The crisp, healing air on Elspeth's face was fresh and smelled of dried leaves, and the sound of roosting crows filled her ears. "Hey!" demanded a third-grader sitting behind them. "Close that...it's too cold!"

"You'll live," Nikki said, without turning her head.

"I'm telling the bus driver!"

"You know, like, this isn't your private limousine, so just *chill,* kid!"

The daily bus trip was only fifteen minutes or so, even with all the stops along the way. Most of the local kids took the bus to school because they didn't want to have to get up any earlier in the morning to walk, but many returned home by foot in small groups.

Five blocks past the old house, the driver parked at the walkway to the school entrance and pulled the lever to open the door, which folded like the bellows of an accordion.

Pausing near the top of the wide granite steps, which took Elspeth an extra minute to climb, Nikki said, "Listen... um...I just wanted to let you know that...well, you're my best friend." She smiled warmly, her braces reflecting the morning sun and causing her friend to squint.

Elspeth tried to smile back, but could only manage a nod of her head. "Thanks. You too."

The abrasive clanging of the bell resonated from within the brooding brick building where four hundred and twelve kids from kindergarten through grade four spent their school days. Nikki said, "Well, see ya at lunch, 'Speth," and they both hastened to the top of the steps and through the doors, heading in different directions to their respective classrooms.

Damon, who was in one of the other fourth grade classrooms, did not join the girls at lunch. In fact, he wasn't even in the lunchroom. "Do you 'spose he's sick?" Elspeth wondered out loud. As she was saying this, something hit the back of her head. She promptly reached behind and found a fistful of instant mashed potato, still warm and oozing with melted butter. At the same time, she could hear subdued laughter from the next table. She stood and turned, staring at the giggling boys and girls, two of whom were in her class. No, she decided. I am *not* going to cry. I am *not* going to lose my temper. I just want to let them know that *I* know who did it.

But Nikki, who was not as discreet, shouted a few very choice and very forbidden words at her friend's tormentors, even as one of the lunch ladies strode with remarkable speed toward her, as though on roller skates. "You come with me right now, young lady," scolded the woman, whose face was flush, like the skin of a tomato. "Empty your tray and come with me. And *you*..." she continued, addressing Elspeth, "you go to the washroom right now and clean that off your hair. Land sakes!"

The lunch lady completely ignored the kids at the next table, who soon were laughing right out loud, not even trying to conceal their glee. "I hear your boyfriend got beat up by his dad last night." Elspeth, standing up with her tray, felt tears collecting in her eyes again, and some real panic. There was nobody there to defend her. "Maybe if you grow another leg, you could help him out!" She emptied her tray into the garbage, including the silverware, and made her way to the girls' washroom, holding her stomach.

Elspeth wound up at the nurse's office shortly after, and her mom picked her up at about one o'clock. She was deeply empty-feeling inside, and angry, but she said nothing about the lunchroom incident. She hadn't time to submit her grammar assignment because English didn't happen until the afternoon. And her hair was still damp on the ride home, which Mom did not notice. "Sorry to make you pick me up."

"Well, when we get home, you'd better hop right into bed. Did you have lunch?"

"Yeah. A hamburger that was...I dunno, like trying to eat a dry sponge."

Trying to cheer her daughter some, her mother said, "I'll bet you haven't tried the really *good* sponges yet." Elspeth shot her a puzzled glance. "There are cherry vanilla ones and butter pecan and a brand new flavor that I think has grape nuts and sprinkles on it. I'll speak to the principal about getting some of those for you guys."

"Mom!" Elspeth giggled, in spite of herself. As they approached the old house at the intersection, her smile flattened. "Mom...pull over for a minute."

"Why? I have to turn here."

"Pl*ease*..."

Mom stopped the car against the curb across from the house and let it idle while her daughter looked past her through the window. "What is it? What are you looking for?"

Elspeth let out a deep sigh. "Could you roll your window down?" Mom was befuddled, but did as requested. After a few silent moments, Elspeth said, "Okay, we can go now."

"Okay," Mom said, with a slight edge of sarcasm mixed equally with concern, "then we're off."

"Mom, can Nikki stay overnight on Friday?"

"That would be all right, I guess, as long as her parents say its okay."

Elspeth was allowed to watch some television that afternoon from the living room couch, with a comforter draped over her. But she wasn't really paying much attention to the shows that were on. She was thinking how great it was going to be if Nikki could spend the night Friday, so they could solidify their trick-or-treat plans. And hopefully, those would include Damon.

And maybe they would stop in front of the house at the corner of Bax and Beechum Streets, and maybe they would hear the dog again. And maybe they'd sneak up to the house, and go inside. And maybe not.

Elspeth felt a bit better now, as she drifted off to sleep on the couch.

When her Dad awakened her for dinner, he told her that she snored.

And that made her laugh for the first time all day.

Chapter 5
Where is Damon?

On Friday, Damon was still a no-show at lunch. It was the topic of much hallway conversation among the older students.

Elspeth and Nikki sat on opposite sides of their table as usual, so that they could look at each other while talking. "Bet you got an 'A' on your English homework, right?" Nikki said.

"I don't know yet. Mrs. Ewell hasn't corrected mine because I left before English period yesterday. How come you weren't on the bus this morning?"

"Oh, Mom had to go to town for an appointment anyway. But, I still get the window seat on Monday."

"Sure. Hey, wanna come over to my house for a sleepover tonight?"

"I'll ask my parents, but they'll probably let me. They always do."

"We can figure out where to trick-or-treat."

"What do ya mean? We're gonna trick-or-treat in the same places we always do. We're only allowed to walk as far as the school and then we have to turn around. That's good enough. I mean, there's about a thousand houses along the way. Plenty of candy."

"Yeah, I 'spose," Elspeth conceded. There was a long silence then, because both girls were thinking the same thing. Elspeth finally said it: "I wonder how

Damon is."

"Must be sick..."

"There was a kid at the next table yesterday who said his dad beat him up."

"Oh, I doubt it," Nikki countered. "Somebody was trying to mess with you. He's probably just sick."

Elspeth suddenly stood from the table, turned to the back of the cafeteria, and walked toward one of the boys' tables.

Alarmed, Nikki called after her. "'Speth! What are you *doing*?"

As Elspeth approached the group of boys with whom Damon usually sat, they all went quiet with bemusement. "Do any of you know where Damon is?"

No one answered the question, but one of them heckled her. "Why? Is he your boyfriend? 'Cause *you're* not his girlfriend. He said so."

Elspeth's eyes narrowed as her brow dropped like a Venetian blind. "I don't care what you think of me. I want to know if Damon's okay. Anyone here brave enough to answer?"

"*Whoa!*" another boy said. "I'd say *you're* the brave one, limping over here without being invited."

"I don't limp. I'll bet I can walk faster than *you* can. So, *where is Damon*?"

A third boy said, quietly, "His dad hit him real bad. He stayed home because he has bruises." The other kids at the table kept silent.

Elspeth sized up the boy, who seemed not to have the judgmental, aggressive look to him that the others had, and asked, "How do you know that?"

"I live right next door to his house. He called me

and told me. He calls me about every day…well, he used to," suddenly turning his head away, he added, "I shouldn't be saying this, because he said he'd get hit again if anyone else found out."

"Oh," Elspeth said, her chin drooping. "Thanks for telling me. I promise I won't say anything." As she turned to leave them, she added, "I'm Elspeth."

"Yeah, I know. *Everyone* knows. I'm Patrick."

The boys' table was quiet as she walked back to sit across from Nikki. "And…?"

"We have to do something."

"About what?" Nikki asked. "Did they threaten you?"

"No, no. One of them told me about Damon. He's hurt. His dad did it."

"Well, what can *we* do…?"

The lunch room proctors were lining up the fourth graders by class, and Elspeth hadn't enough time to finish her tuna sandwich. She stuffed it carelessly into her pocket.

"Talk to ya later."

"Yup, later."

Later was 3:15 that afternoon, when the bell rang to end the school day. The two girls hooked up at the bottom of the granite steps and began their thirty-eighth walk home that school year. The sky was overcast and there was the smokeless scent of burning leaves drifting in from somewhere, which was a lovely, homey smell.

They were talking about Damon, and about what two ten-year-old girls might do to help him, when they reached the corner of Bax and Beechum Streets. And the house. They stopped, faced the building, and listened intently.

Nothing.

Oh, a siren passing by. A person shouting from across the street. As usual, the leaves tittering in the light autumn breeze, a few more breaking away from their branches to spiral toward the ground.

But nothing else. Nothing that Elspeth and Nikki were listening for, at any rate.

"You know what? When we thought we heard something on Tuesday, I'll bet we were imagining it," Nikki said. "Or it was just some dog *behind* the house that sounded like it could be inside. We didn't hear it ever before, and we haven't heard it since."

Elspeth did not want to admit that her friend was probably right. However, it was rather heartbreaking for her to think that a lonely, starving dog might be in that house. If there was, someone ought to rescue it. *She* should rescue it, she decided. "Well, I think there's a dog in there. Might be real, might be..."

"What, like, a ghost? Well, I don't really believe in ghosts, but I do believe in *real* dogs."

"Well, duh!" Elspeth said, instantly regretting her sarcasm. She let the soft breeze blow her hair into her face, where it curled around her mouth and nose, as she continued to listen intently for a sign to confirm the existence of the animal both girls thought they'd heard on Tuesday. Finally defeated, they turned and headed around the corner onto Beechum Street.

There was the hint of much colder weather in the air. In less than a month, there could be snow.

"So, what can we do about Damon?" Elspeth asked again. Then she said, "Ew, gross!" as she withdrew her hand from her pants pocket and found it full of tuna fish and squashed remnants of bread. "I forgot all about the sandwich! Yuck!"

"It still looks better than what we get on our trays a lot of days! Anyway, we can talk about Damon when I sleep over tomorrow. *If* I can come."

Having no other answer between them, the girls continued on to their homes.

Chapter 6
Over Night Mare

Elspeth was excited to have Nikki over Friday night. There is always something liberating and adventurous about sleeping over at a friend's house. Kids can usually stay up half the night as long as they whispered, and watch horror movies and gossip and make all kinds of plans. They have tremendous fun, sharing secrets and being a bit loud (often a bit obnoxious), but never quite getting into mischief.

On this Friday, just five nights from Halloween, Mom let them order a pizza, and after supper they scurried to the basement, where there was a ping pong table, shelves supporting paint cans and tools along one wall, and a puffy bean bag seats in front of a television. "I still can't believe you have *two TV*s."

"Yeah, this is the smaller one."

"We just have one, and we're always arguing about who gets to pick a show. Are your parents rich?"

Elspeth hadn't ever thought about it. "I don't think so. Dad sells houses and I guess he makes pretty good money. Mom doesn't really have to work, but she volunteers in the library once or twice a week."

"My dad's in charge of the deli department at Cavender's. Mom is...well, she's, like, a cleaner. She goes into other people's houses and cleans."

"Yeah, you told me. I'll bet she's great at it."

"But it's funny, because our house is messy most of the time."

Elspeth's father came down the steps to the basement and found her and Nikki lounged in the bean bags, sort-of watching comedy shows, but mostly talking with each other about girl stuff. "Hello, Nikki," he said, with a welcoming smile.

"Hi, Mr. Amesbury. Thank you for letting me stay here tonight."

"It's our pleasure," he said, grabbing something from the chest freezer before heading back upstairs.

"Wanna play a game or something?" Elspeth asked, in the middle of a yawn.

But they were both sleepy, and retired to Elspeth's room instead. Her wallpaper was a pattern of flower bouquets and tiny kittens against a pastel blue background that Elspeth found restful. Most of her toys, which should have been on her shelves or in the closet, were crammed under her bed along with her old crutch, which she still used to go to the bathroom without having to put her leg on. Only an array of particular furry animals was allowed on top. Elspeth picked up a soft stuffed bunny from her pillow and hugged it. "Feel this. Feel the fur."

"Oh, awesome!"

"Here...I'll let you borrow him tonight if you want," she offered, reaching to pass it across to Nikki, who hesitated. "Don't worry...I have lots of other animals. But Jumper is my favorite. I named him Jumper because I make him hop really high," she explained, demonstrating by lifting her hand over her head then dropping it down to the bed over and over, as the rabbit's ears flopped wildly. "Here, take him."

"Thanks!" Nikki said, with a broad, grateful smile. "My favorite stuffed animal in my room is Yertle. He's a turtle that I carry around all the time at home. I named him after that Dr. Seuss book. He has brown and white spots all over his back and a big weird head that looks like a log. I'll show him to you if you'll ever come to my house. How come you don't come when I invite you?"

Elspeth diverted Nikki's attention from the subject, "Hey, Nik, let's make a tent tonight!"

The girls looked at each other and grinned as though they were about to do something fun but borderline prohibited. Stripping the two blankets and sheets from Elspeth's bed, they shook them flat, giggling as they draped them over furniture, watching their structure grow bigger and bigger, taking on a crazy shape. It fell in a few times as they tried to secure the corners to shelves, a table and a desk using knots or heavy school books. Once, as it was collapsing, Lucie flew terrified from under a blanket and through the door into the hall like a subliminal streak of gray and white. Elspeth couldn't stop laughing. "I didn't know she was under there!" This was so much fun, the girls wondered why they hadn't thought to do it before.

"I have a *real* tent, 'Speth! Dad bought it for me to use when we all went camping, except that we didn't go camping at all last summer. Too much rain."

Now Elspeth needed to remove her prosthetic leg before they prepared to bed down in their sleeping bags. Nikki had watched her do this several times, always with a combination of fascination, sadness and horror as her best friend sat flat on the floor and turned down an outer sleeve covering part of her right leg. She then dislodged herself from a long plastic shell that had a short silver pole where her ankle should be. The foot was made from wood, with a hard foam surface that was shaped like toes at its end. Below the base of her real knee was a stump of healed-over skin, which had been protected by two or three layers of special socks, now removed.

Elspeth noticed Nikki's usual wide-eyed look. "I told you, Nik, it doesn't hurt. Only for a while after the surgery. *Looks* a little gross, I guess. But, hey, I'm part-robot now! Isn't that cool?"

"Except that it smells like the bottom of my hamster cage. And how come going upstairs to your room doesn't bother you, but getting on the bus is so hard?"

"The bus steps are a lot steeper. Actually, going up to my room was hard at first, too. Dad had to carry me upstairs for about a month. Then I used a crutch with one hand and held the railing with the other. But I practiced a lot and now it's pretty easy. I could even ride a bike...if I *had* a bike...or go swimming if I wanted to. Maybe I will next summer."

"I like going swimming, but if I had a fake leg, I think it would be embarrassing to wear a bathing suit around people, 'cause kids would make fun of me. Well, they already do anyway. Just not for *that*. You know...tinsel teeth and stuff."

"You'll be done with your braces some day, but I'll never grow another real leg. And I think you're really pretty, Nik, even with your braces."

"You do?"

"Yeah. You have such beautiful hair with all those waves, and your brown eyes are almost black. I think you could be a model some day. I feel jealous of you sometimes."

"Wow. You never told me that before. I've always thought that *you* were really pretty because you're a blonde, and I was kinda ugly."

"Uh-uh. *I'm* the ugly one. This stupid leg. Probably this sounds weird, but for a while after it stopped hurting four years ago, I was almost glad about the accident because Mom and Dad paid attention to me *all* the time. They took me lots of places to cheer me up, like Disney World, and they got Lucie from the shelter to keep me company. But now, I just think I look horrible. Want some cheese puffs?"

Reaching into the bag being held out to her, Nikki nodded toward Elspeth's stump and asked, "How did that accident happen? You never told me much about it."

"You never asked before."

"Never seemed polite. But I've always wanted to know."

"You're my best friend, so I don't mind if you know. Just don't spread it around, okay? I was in the back seat and some lady drove her pickup into the side of our car where I was sitting. She went right through a red light. She got a con...concon...no, a con*cussion*. Mom had a broken arm. Dad wasn't hurt at all. But my leg got crushed and they had to take it off. And one side of my face got messed up," she said, pointing to the right side of her mouth, where her dimple appeared when she smiled.

Nikki held back her tears, and her voice was

unsteady. "Jeez, 'Speth."

"Don't feel sorry for me. C'mon. You've known me for years and you know I can walk almost like a regular person. But anyway, good. Now you know."

An old silver flashlight was used to illuminate their cave-like creation. Elspeth had her own sleeping bag for camping, which she had taken from her closet, and had borrowed her Mom's for Nikki to use. They were placed side-by-side on the floor, and fit easily beneath the crazy canopy. By now in their pajamas, they lay on their stomachs with their legs up, developing plans for the coming Halloween night. Their faces were contoured with improbable shadows from the flashlight on the floor between them, making them appear chalky and ghoulish.

"I *was* going to go as Wonder Woman," Nikki said, "but I changed my mind. Now my mom is going to make me up to look like the Wicked Witch from *The Wizard of Oz.*"

"I've seen it a billion times. That's a good idea. But what will she use to make your face green? Maybe you could just eat more school food than usual that day! Anyway, I'm still going as a vampire. I have the teeth already. Wanna see 'em?"

"It's okay. I believe you."

There was a lengthy lull in the conversation. Then: "Hey, Nik...what are we gonna do?"

"Well, just go to sleep, I guess...I'm tired," her friend replied, scratching Lucie's white tummy as the cat lay on her back, her eyes in a blissful squint and two front paws bent in carefree submission.

"No, no...I mean, about Damon." Elspeth said.

"What *can* we do? If he's not going with us, he's

not going with us. He's been out of school for days."

"I wish we could..." Elspeth's voice trailed off, a vacant expression taking over her face.

"We can't help him, 'Speth, even if those guys in the cafeteria were telling the truth. I mean, we're just *girls*."

"Girls can do anything boys can, Nik! What if we told grown-ups about what I heard? Wouldn't they have to...I dunno, investigate or something? I think my mom and dad would do something about it. Call somebody..."

"You're really into this, aren't you?"

"He's our *friend*, Nik! And even if he wasn't..."

"He'll be okay. What proof do you have of what those boys said, anyway?"

"Why are you so sure he'll be okay?" Elspeth answered, increasingly peeved. "And just so you know, it wasn't *all* the boys. It was just Patrick."

"Who's Patrick?"

"I don't know him, but he was the only one at the table who gave me an answer. And another thing – what about the house?"

"The house? You mean the corner house? What about it?"

"What if we hear a dog in there crying again while we're trick-or-treating?" Elspeth asked.

"Then we should walk away really, *really* fast!"

"I think we should go to the house. You know, maybe not go *in* it, but get up close and whistle or something. Maybe it would come to us."

"You're bonkers! I'm not going any closer than, like, the sidewalk."

"But what if it sounds like it's in pain? Maybe it's

abandoned and lying hurt in there."

The girls kept on with this for a time, going around and around and coming up with no resolve. Elspeth asked Nikki to go to the switch by the door and turn off the room light, leaving the door open a crack so that Lucie could wander in and out. Most nights, the cat would jump on Elspeth's bed and snuggle, purring, against the back of Elspeth's neck. Sure enough, the cat soon poked through the tent wall and curled up between the girls, who by then were sound asleep in their homemade tent, having accidently left the flashlight on.

Elspeth was buckled in and watching the scenery go by. It was going to be a good day. The family was headed to see her uncle Leland, who was her dad's brother, in North Conway. That was always a fun trip, as she was doted upon by Uncle Leland and Aunt Chrissie, who had a swimming pool and offered her unlimited chocolate chip cookies.

Out of the corner of her eye, she saw something in the window that should not have been there... a huge, dark shape heading directly toward her. The second she turned her head to look at it directly, there was a tremendous blast of glass shards that went everywhere, cutting her arm and face. She felt great pressure on her right leg, though no immediate pain. She was aware that their car was being propelled sideways, no longer moving forward. Her dad was shouting, "Hang on!" as he struggled with the steering wheel, and her mother was screaming. Elspeth made no sound whatsoever until the car came to a standstill and the pain began to overtake her, and then began crying hysterically.

And that was what Elspeth dreamed on the night when Nikki slept over, and on many other nights before that one. This time, the nightmare did not end even after she realized she was safe in her bedroom, in a makeshift tent, with a friend sleeping beside her. The flashlight had gone dark, but she knew, as she felt wetness inside her sleeping bag that had a familiar odor, that she needed dry clothes right away. She crawled from the tent, dragging her sleeping bag out with her and, in the dim glow from the night light near the door and her bedside alarm clock, slid silently into her artificial leg, careful not to disturb Nikki. She made her way to the door of her parents' room, feeling her way along the hallway wall, and quietly slipping inside. "Mom? Dad? I need help."

Chapter 7
Saturday

When Nikki woke, she found Elspeth was not with her in the tent. The bedroom window was letting the sunless gray of a heavily overcast morning seep in, heartened only by the chirps of a nearby cardinal. Sitting up, she breathed in the smell of bacon, toast, and coffee. She unzipped her bag and climbed out, put on her slippers and tiptoed down the stairs to find her friend.

Elspeth was already dressed and sitting at the table, and gave Nikki a wide smile. "Hello! Sorry I came down before you, but I was awake early and I didn't want to bother you."

Mom said to Nikki, "Hope you're hungry."

"I could eat, like, ten pizzas right now!"

"Well, you girls already had your pizza last night. How do you want your eggs, Nikki?"

"She likes them cooked," said Elspeth, with a grin.

"Well, I'll just scramble them this morning."

Lucie stood on the chair beside Elspeth, her front paws up on the edge of the table and her little black nose poised in the air, sniffing longingly of the perfume rising from hot bacon on a plate, which was within her reach. "Hey! I already fed you! Get down!" Elspeth commanded, shooing the cat, who landed with a thud on the linoleum. "Jeez. She doesn't learn *any*thing."

"Well, 'Speth, I mean, wouldn't *you* rather have bacon than the same old boring food you get out of a can every day?" Nikki asked.

"What are you girls going to do today?"

"What do you want to do, 'Speth?"

"Can we go see a movie?"

"It's supposed to be sunny and warm out. Why not do something outside?" Mom asked.

"But can't we go to a movie? I haven't been to one for a long time."

"Well...Nikki, what time do you have to be home, dear?"

"I just have to be home by dinner."

"And what is showing at the matinee?" Siteson's small movie theater actually still offered weekend matinees for kids.

The Saturday paper said it was *Journey to the Outer Galaxy*. "Cool...science-fiction! Maybe it'll have monsters!"

The girls were each given money to get them into the theater, and enough leftover to buy a snack. They had to stand in a rather lengthy line made up of kids eager to get out of the lovely autumn sun and into a stuffy, dark auditorium where they could throw popcorn at each other. The aisle floor was sticky, and Nikki found a wad of chewed gum stuck to her chair arm. "Don't they ever clean this place?"

First, there was a preview of next week's Saturday matinee, which was an older movie called *The Hound of the Baskervilles*. It looked scary enough so that Nikki had to look down from the screen. At one moment, two men were holding a candle while they stood at the window of a huge mansion, looking out into the night. Then came a most frightening howl.

"I gotta go to the bathroom," Elspeth said, walking sideways to the aisle through a sea of legs, and then to the back of the theater, before returning some minutes later after the preview had ended and a cartoon started. Again, she had to make about ten kids move their legs to the side to let her by. Settling back into her seat, she wondered if seeing a preview with a scary dog on this particular weekend was simply a coincidence, or maybe some kind of sign. An omen. A jinx.

She did not mention this to Nikki as they left the theater, squinting from the sudden blinding sun, waiting on the sidewalk for Dad to pick them up. Instead, she said, "That was a dumb movie."

"I liked it. Kinda cool special effects."

"But you could see the wires holding up the spaceship. Someday, I'm gonna make my own movie, and it'll be better than that one."

"Hey, 'Speth – isn't that Damon?"

"What?"

"Damon. Isn't that Damon walking with those boys down the street? I'll bet he was in the theater with us."

From behind, Elspeth saw a tangerine-headed boy amongst three or four other kids as he headed away from them along the sidewalk. "I can't tell. I hope so. I hope he's okay."

Elspeth's dad dropped Nikki off at her house after the movie.

"Thanks, Daddy," Elspeth said.

"You're welcome...but what for?"

"Well, for driving us to the movie. And, you know, for last night."

Dad's head nodded in front of her. "Oh, Little Squirrel, I used to wet my bed too, sometimes. It seemed like the most horrible thing that could happen, but as I got older, it stopped. You'll be okay."

"Anyway, thanks for making sure Nikki didn't find out. But that's why I don't want to sleep over at her house."

Dad smiled at her from the rear-view mirror. "Mom did most of the work. But, you're welcome." That was all Elspeth needed then to make her feel important and loved.

Chapter 8
A Few Good Moments

On Monday, it rained, and it was chilly. There were gusts of wind that brought with them the sweet-and-sour odor of damp leaves and wood smoke. Children who had planned to trick-or-treat in two days were worried the weather would not get better in time, because carrying an umbrella while knocking on dozens of front doors was just not as much fun. And most would have to be driven by grown-ups from house to house, taking even more of the spooky magic away.

Mom suggested she drive Elspeth to school, as she always offered to do when it rained or snowed or was below-zero cold, which would save her daughter from having to stand at the curb for the bus. On such days, she would take the bus home when school let out.

But days like this made Elspeth – and probably many kids while at school – a little depressed. Sitting in her classroom that morning, she kept glancing out the window and focusing on the sinewy empty branches of the oak trees that surrounded the school, looking somewhat distorted through the veil of diagonal rain. The classroom itself was darker than usual and strange, like it was raining *in* the room but not really. The nights when parents brought their children to the school for an open house every year were like this – a bit otherworldly. Just not normal.

Worse still, of course, was that there would be no outdoor recess, and everyone would be sitting at their desks and coloring or making origami airplanes and poppers and fortune tellers, or just getting up and mulling aimlessly around the room, chatting to friends along the way.

Elspeth did not have a lot of real friends, and the only one she was really close to wasn't even in her class. And there was Damon, who she wanted to know better but who also wasn't in her class. It was true that most students did not pick on her, and some were usually polite and even open to being her friend, but she did not seem to want to talk about herself. So, recess on rainy days was awkward for her as she tried to stay invisible by reading a book she liked, afraid someone would snicker about her leg, whispering about her just loudly enough so she could hear.

Her teacher was well aware of how funereal this kind of day was, and usually tried to inject a bit of levity into her lessons. The first thing Mrs. Ewell did that Monday morning, after saying, "Good morning, everyone," was to get right into posing a challenge to her class. "Boys and girls, for the math part of your morning, I want you all to solve the following word problem."

The class laid fresh pieces of lined, hole-punched notebook paper in front of them, and had their number 2 pencils at the ready.

Mrs. Ewell began: "Johnny had three apples. They were ripe and juicy. Two friends of Johnny's came over. Johnny gave each of them one of his apples. Then another friend of Johnny's came over and asked if he could have an apple, so Johnny gave him his last one. Then, Johnny regretted giving everything away, and asked one of his friends if he could have half of one of their apples back. But his friends were hungry, and two of them broke their apples into quarters instead of halves, offering him one. Then, another friend came over with a bag full of fireballs. If two of Johnny's friends broke their apples into quarters, and Johnny got two quarters, and the third friend didn't break his apple at all...*how many fireballs does the fourth friend have in his bag?*"

The class was silent, looking at each other and shrugging their shoulders in frustration. Then, Elspeth started to laugh, and Mrs. Ewell laughed, and finally, everyone in the class laughed.

The one other pleasant break from this otherwise bleak Monday was lunch period. Pleasant, because Damon showed up.

He sat with the girls this time, putting his tray of meat loaf, corn and white rice with gravy in front of him with a pronounced clash. "Hey," he said, nonchalantly.

"Hey!" Elspeth replied, smiling broadly. Dampening this reunion a bit was the fact that she thought she could detect some redness and swelling on his cheek and chin, but did not mention it.

"I'm going with you guys Wednesday night," he said, rather solemnly.

Elspeth could hardly contain her joy. "Oh, cool! It's the three of us, then."

Damon seemed a little different...rather distant. His usual upbeat countenance was tamped-down. He was pensive and did not look the girls in the eye as much as usual, instead forking up and eating his food as though no one else was there.

The girls both noticed this right away and tried to find thoughtful ways of talking to him. Nikki said, "We're glad you're back. Were you very sick?"

Without glancing up from his food, Damon said, "I wasn't sick. But thanks for asking."

"Who are you going to go trick-or-treating as?" Elspeth asked.

"Um...a vampire, I guess."

"Oh." Elspeth said, with a slightly panicked face aimed at Nikki across the table.

For the first time, Damon looked at Elspeth directly. "What?"

"Well, no, that's okay. I mean...I was going as a vampire, too."

"So? Can't two vampires travel together? What are you gonna be, Nikki?"

"The Wicked Witch of the West."

Damon actually almost cracked a smile. "So, perfect! Who *says* that Oz didn't have vampires in it? We both went to see The Wizard and he gave us fangs. Perfect."

This cheered the girls to the point of laughing.

It was settled, then. Damon would meet the girls by the school at five o'clock Wednesday afternoon, and the three of them would haunt the neighborhood as the Wicked Witch and her two vampire friends.

Chapter 9
The Big Day Before the Big Night

Aside from Christmas, or Hanukkah, or maybe birthdays, Halloween rules the kid calendar. Much of the entire month of October is centered on how to best accumulate mountains of candy, and on how to make the night scary, but not *really* scary. Chasing after other kids one might meet along the way was always fun: some would carry squirt guns or colored string that fired out from a nozzle, or even explode firecrackers that their parents didn't know about.

The kids whose parents didn't have a lot of money were usually dressed in five-dollar costumes that came in boxes, including flimsy plastic masks that only had tiny holes for eyes and mouth, with rubber bands that always – *always* – broke or pulled out of their staples, forcing the wearers to hold them up to their faces at every door. Others had expensive, full-head rubber masks of horror monsters like werewolves or mummies, but they were hot to wear and got all wet inside from breath. And, there were those wearing homemade costumes and make-up provided by parents who well-remembered how much fun Halloween was for young people. Those were the kids who felt most comfortable as they traversed the night, for they could both see *and* breathe. Nikki and Elspeth would be among those more fortunate ones.

As luck would have it, the rain disappeared early on Tuesday afternoon, and the sun poked out a little. Elspeth and Nikki could walk home after all. And, as they did so, their conversation was light and full of laughter.

Then they reached the corner. And the house.

The girls were about to simply walk right by it, having earlier decided that nothing was going to happen there anymore.

But then, something *did* happen there.

Slowly protruding from one of the broken windows on the second floor was the snout of an animal. It was brownish, and long, with a black, canine nose. As Elspeth and Nikki squinted to see better from way back on the sidewalk, the face shifted to the side a bit, then pulled back into the house, out of sight. "Oh...my...god," Nikki said, her voice quavering. Then, from inside the house, there emerged the howling of an animal, like the one in the movie preview on Saturday. But maybe it was a wolf. Or *something*.

"See?" Elspeth insisted. "*You* saw it, too, right?"

Nikki was coming a bit unglued and was squeezing Elspeth's arm for support. "Let's get home. Come on, 'Speth!"

"Hold on. It can't hurt us from in there! We need to help it."

"What? *Help* it? You're losing it, girl!"

"We should call the animal department at the police."

"But what if they come over here and, like, don't find anything? We'll look like idiots!" she said, pulling on Elspeth's shirt sleeve.

"Please don't do that. And, *so what* if we look like idiots? Wouldn't be the first time."

"'Speth, whatever is in there, we can't help. It's maybe a wild animal with rabies and it could be really dangerous. Or it could be a monster dog like the Baskervilles one. If *you* wanna help it, fine, but I'm not having anything to do with..."

"Shh!" Elspeth said, and both girls froze. The howling became a pathetic moan, like a creature dying and begging for someone to come to its rescue. "See? It wants help."

"*Or* it's trying to lure us...make us feel sorry for it so we'll go in there and be its next meal!"

"That is really stupid. I think it *needs* us."

"Needs *you*, maybe. I'm telling you, this is creepy. I say, let's just stay out of it."

"Yeah, like you wanted to stay out of trying to help Damon. What's *wrong* with you?"

Nikki wordlessly turned and walked away from Elspeth toward home. Elspeth watched her go and did not try to catch up. Instead, she just stared at the house for a long while, knowing that she was going to approach it Wednesday night, *if* she could persuade Damon to go with her.

That afternoon in her bedroom, Elspeth cleared off three shelves of books and magazines in preparation for the candy she would soon have. The top shelf was for the best of the best: the *full-size* candy bars like the ones at the supermarket cash registers. One shelf down was for bite-size candy that you could buy in big bags, plus candied apples and the best not-candy good stuff. At the bottom, everything else would be sorted out: small bags of candy corn, popcorn balls, those orange marshmallow peanut things, licorice twizzles (both red and black), lollipops, bubble gum, little red jelly fish, chocolate kisses and all manner of chewies, crunchies, gooeys and gummies.

She had her bag ready – it was a big, reusable shopping bag that could probably fit about three thousand candy bars, with a picture of a black cat arching its back while standing atop a carved pumpkin. Posing before the front of the full-length mirror in her parents' room, she tried on the shirt that she'd picked out at the store, and the black cape lined with red that Mom had made just for tomorrow night.

When Dad came home, she made mention of the dog she had both seen and heard that afternoon. "Well," he said, "that building is probably pretty easy for animals to get into, so..."

"But, Dad, it's probably been locked up in there for twenty years or something."

"Oh, no. Dogs just don't live that long."

"But maybe this one isn't even alive. It could be a ghost dog."

"Oh, Little Squirrel, I know it's fun to pretend..."

"*Dad*!" Elspeth said in a loud voice, growing frustrated and sliding off her Daddy's lap. "I'm tired of people not believing me about stuff!"

"Time to eat," Mom said. "Elspeth, come feed Lucie first."

At the table, the dog conversation continued. "I think someone ought to help it out."

Dad put down his knife and fork. "I believe you saw *a* dog and heard *a* dog," he said. "Probably just a stray critter who uses the old house for shelter."

Elspeth stood from her chair and put her dishes on

the counter. Defiantly, she then walked to the stairs leading to her bedroom, saying, "Well, *I'm* gonna find out."

"Wait," her dad commanded, and Elspeth stopped on the fourth stair without turning around. "Listen, now: I do *not* want you breaking into that house. It's old and it hasn't been kept up. You could fall through the floor, step on a rusty nail or knock something loose or...besides, it's against the law to trespass."

"All right," Elspeth said, knowing that Dad would keep her home on Halloween if she insisted on going to the house. "But I wasn't imagining anything. Just ask Nikki."

She decided to go to bed early, without waiting to be tucked in.

Elspeth had her right leg back. She was running from lawn to lawn with friends, swinging her trick-or-treat bag to and fro. In a flash, it was spring and she was chasing fireflies, catching a dozen in a jar, then letting them go. Suddenly, she was swimming in the lake all the way from the dock to the buoy rope, her two perfect legs propelling her like the fins of a dolphin. Then, music played. It was her favorite song from the radio. She danced to it somewhere under a spotlight on an enormous stage. Her right knee bent upward and her foot kicked outwards as she stretched her arms straight ahead. Suddenly she was holding her stuffed rabbit Jumper and the two twirled and swirled, laughing and singing along with the song. Damon appeared and became her dancing partner.

In bed, still fast asleep, her eyes moved back and

forth beneath her lids, and she had a wide smile on her mouth.

At a little after eleven, she awoke. She wanted to go back to sleep. She didn't want the dream to end...it had seemed so lovely and real. She pondered why the good dreams were so short and the horrible ones went on forever. Then, through the crack in her door she heard her parents' voices. They were arguing downstairs. She could not understand what they were saying, except that she heard her name mentioned several times, which flooded her with fear. What had she done? She reached under her bed and pulled out her crutch, and tried her hardest to move silently as she made her careful way down the first few stairs at the end of the hall. There she sat, holding onto the banister posts as she pushed her face between them, trying to hear better.

"I'm just afraid that she's reliving past issues right now, like all the old stuff is coming back...wetting her bed and imagining that she..."

"Come on, Ray...she's doing just fine! I think she just had a nightmare on Friday. And she sounds like she just wants to help a stray dog that might be living in that house. I think she's being really sweet about it. She has compassion. Not every kid has that."

"Yes, I know, Sally. She's a wonderful kid, but..."

"You still can't forgive yourself about her leg."

"Keep it down. She might be able to hear you."

"She's *all right*. Kids have dreams. Kids wet beds. Kids have imaginary friends."

"But not all kids lose a leg."

"Well, *our* child did, and she's coping with it amazingly well. Come on, Ray, she just loves you so much, she thinks you're a superhero. Please don't disappoint her. She needs your support."

"I *always* give her support, Sal. Don't I? Sal?" The absence of a reply seemed to further agitate him. "But, well...how come she only has one friend in the whole school?"

"She has two. She mentioned a boy named Damon. All three of them are trick-or-treating tomorrow."

"Damon? I don't know anything about him. Okay, so that makes two friends. Only *two*. I think we ought to take her to a psychologist or the school nurse or *somebody*. Don't you think?"

By this time, Elspeth was silently sobbing, pursing her lips and wiping her eyes with her arm, but she couldn't stop listening. This was like when she was six, just after the accident, and for a whole year after. And now it was back again: her parents were yelling at each other and it always had something to do with her.

Chapter 10
Memento mori

Mom used her own makeup to turn Elspeth's face a very pale white, the color of a zombie. Bright red lipstick, some shadow under the eyes and a thickening of her eyebrows with liner perfectly complemented the plastic fangs. "You look really good," her mother said.

"Mom, do you think I'm pretty?"

"The way you look now, or the way you usually look?"

"Well," she answered with a chuckle, "not the way I look *now*..."

"I think you're perfect, sweetie. You were blessed with lovely blonde hair and blue eyes, and in truth I've always loved your dimple. Of course, you look like your dad, so I'm a little biased. Why do you ask?"

"Just wondering."

"You're going to break a few hearts one day."

"No...probably just my own. I don't think any boys will like me when they find out I'm missing a leg."

"That's just silly, Elspeth. Does Damon like you?"

"Um, I guess he does..."

"Does he know you wear a prosthesis?"

"Uh-huh."

"There you go, then. A lot of people can see right

past that kind of thing. Listen, you are a *whole person*. You're smart and kind and brave – and that's what people will see most as you grow up. Trust me."

Elspeth stood before the glass door of the microwave and studied her reflection. She looked awesome. "*But*," she said, suddenly spinning around toward her mom with her fangs open wide and curled fingers held up in a threatening posture, "I'm not *always* kind...sometimes I drink blood!" She couldn't wait for Nikki and Damon to see her scary disguise. "Thanks, Mom!"

Desperately wanting to bring up the subject of her parents' argument the previous night, but worrying she might not get a really honest answer (or maybe that she would), she kept it to herself. Stirring in her memory were the explanations she'd been given four years ago when she'd brought this up, such as, "Oh, sweetie, we just had a disagreement. Grown-ups have them all the time, but they manage to get over them," she'd been told.

"But, Mom," she had said in return, "I want you and Dad to stay together!" Nothing her parents had told her back then about their arguing comforted her.

Even now, four years later, Elspeth blamed herself for most everything bad that happened, even when something wasn't *her* fault, because that's what kids do. And *certainly* she'd been the one who had caused that argument just last night after she'd thrown a tantrum about the dog in the old house.

But, this being Halloween, she decided to try to put all of that aside so that she could enjoy her time with her friends that night.

Dad dropped the girls off at the school while it was still light. Damon was waiting for them. He was wearing a five-dollar Dracula costume and a cheesy plastic mask that had a rubber band. After the girls got out of the car, Dad said, "Hello. You must be Damon."

"Uh-huh."

"Well, you kids have fun, but be careful tonight. And Damon, these girls are *not* to go near that old house, do you understand?" he asked, sternly.

"Okay," Damon told him.

"All right. Be home before eight, girls."

"Yeah, Dad. We'll be on time. Promise." As her father turned around and slowly pulled away, Elspeth said, "Jeez, he's not usually this...I dunno... Anyway, let's go!"

Nikki's green face and hands were colorless in the night, except when she passed beneath the street lights. Her tall, pointed hat kept wanting to slide off her head, and she had to constantly reposition it. Damon had his mask down around his neck between houses. Elspeth had pocketed her fangs so that she could talk to her friends. And the three began their walk to the corner.

The air was humming with voices and laughter from unseen little kids. Mixing with the wonderful smell of someone's chimney smoke was the aroma of candle-lit pumpkins and, when the wind blew just so, the crisp, fresh, almost-November air just ahead of winter.

Since the houses were close together on Bax Street, but not so close on Beechum, most of their candy was going to be collected before they reached the corner.

When the kids knocked on the door of one house, an elderly woman with a bun in her hair opened the door, holding a wicker basket. "Oh, my...don't you all look scary! Well, if you do a trick, I will give you a treat."

Damon whispered to his friends, "What? We never had to do *this* before."

"Like, what *kind* of trick?" Nikki asked of the lady.

"Well...how about all of you pretending you're little doggies and barking and begging like you want a biscuit!"

Under his breath, Damon mumbled, "Oh, brother! And after we do this, she'll probably give us dog biscuits instead of candy!"

The three children bent their wrists like they were puppies standing on their hind legs, and began whimpering and yipping as best they could. It would have looked very strange to see two vampires and a wicked witch pleading for treats like starving puppies. It was beneath their dignity but, hey, it was for candy.

"Oh, that's just wonderful!" the lady said. "Here...you may each take two."

Two bite-size candies plopped into each of their three bags. "Thank you!" they said, almost in unison, and made their way back to the sidewalk.

"That was *awful*!" Nikki said.

"Well, it's okay," Elspeth pointed out, "I'm sure that's the only place we'll have to do that. Plus, we already have a lot of candy."

As they continued along, they passed by a couple of other groups of kids. In one of them, someone was holding a burning gold sparkler, and another was all lit up with blinking colored lights, which covered his clown costume and even his oversized shoes. Elspeth didn't think that any of them had costumes or make-up as good as theirs. And, because nobody sprayed anything on each other or tried to pick a fight, it was a fairly uneventful walk so far.

The three were constantly crossing and re-crossing the street in order to hit every house. A pair of teenagers wearing zombie make-up had just stepped away from a home decorated with dozens of little facial-tissue ghosts tied to tree branches and bushes, and were about to pass them on the walkway. "Don't go there," one of the zombie girls said. "Skip this one."

Damon asked, "Why?"

"Not worth it. Too weird."

"Is she giving out good stuff?"

"It's okay. Big candy bars, but still not worth it. Where're you guys from?"

"Beechum and Bax. Right around here. You?"

"We're from Lennington, actually, but there are more houses here than in our hood."

"Yeah, well," Damon continued, "thanks for telling us." The two groups parted, and Elspeth, Nikki and Damon continued on toward the house in spite of the warning. "Big candy bars. What's not to like? But I don't remember this house from last year, do you?"

The porch was lit with a single orange light bulb. Huge pumpkins on either side of the door were carved with threatening eyes and gnarly, toothy grins, looking like they could suddenly come to life and take massive bites out of the kids' ankles and legs. Damon used the door knocker, which he was pretty sure was the *only* door knocker in the neighborhood.

The door creaked open. Yes, it creaked, like a scary

movie door would. Inside, there stood a woman all hunched over and wearing a florid dress and ornate bracelets and many strands of beads. There was only a single deep-red light inside, making it hard to see her face. "Come in," she said. The three glanced at each other, and Damon shrugged his shoulders, stepping into the foyer ahead of the girls. Elspeth thought she saw something low to the floor moving beside them, and squinted. There appeared to be a transparent outline, reddish in the light, cloud-like and inconstant. She rubbed her eyes, smearing her makeup a little, but the wispy outline was gone.

Once inside, the door was shut behind them. Nikki grabbed Elspeth's arm. "There's a skull. A *skull*!" Elspeth and Damon looked to where she was pointing and there, red as blood under the foyer light, rested an animal skull on a small table. "Is that real?"

"Oh, my, yes," croaked the old woman with a voice Damon thought was an obvious put-on just to creep them out. "Who wants to hold it?"

"I will," Damon said, allowing the old woman to put the skull into his hands. The eyes and nose were hollow, but its needle-like teeth were still very much intact. "Cool!" he said, holding the face of the skull to within a few inches of his face. He sniffed it, to see if it had an odor.

"That's gross, Damon," Nikki scolded.

"Memento mori," the woman said.

"What does that mean?" Elspeth asked.

"This skull was once underneath the skin of a dog," she said, looking at Damon. "Hand it back to me, son," she said, and Damon returned it to her hands.

"How did you get it?" he asked.

"You know the old house on the corner? The big yellow one?"

"Yeah, we know it," Elspeth said, as her friends nodded in agreement.

"I used to go there every few weeks and take out the weeds. Ya know, place looked bad from the sidewalk with all those big ol' stalks growing wild and all. One day about a month ago, I spotted this skull near the house, half sticking out of the ground. Never found any bones or nothin', just this. I cleaned it all up and gave it a shine. Been keepin' me company ever since, smilin' at me from the table."

Nikki decided she wanted out and turned to leave, with or without her friends.

"Now, now, little one," the woman said to her. "Nothing here's gonna hurt you."

Nikki whispered, "Let's go, *please*."

"Jeez, Nik, you always just want to go home from everywhere," Elspeth remarked.

The woman went on: "Memento mori. It's Latin for 'Remember, you must die.' That means you better enjoy your life, because, no matter how old or young you are, you...and all of us...will be gone one day. Maybe you get sick, maybe you have an accident." Elspeth winced, trying to keep memories of the car crash from rushing in. "And we probably won't see it coming. And maybe one day, *your* skulls will be keeping watch in someone's house."

Nikki shook her head violently, and Elspeth said, "We should go now. Thank you."

"Of course." The woman returned the skull to the table as Nikki opened her front door and hurried through it toward the sidewalk, followed by her friends. "But...don't you want your treats?" the woman called, holding a basket out in front of her.

"No, thank you," Elspeth shouted over her shoulder.

"I'll get 'em," Damon said, and ran back to the door, taking a fistful of candy bars. As he caught up to his friends, he asked, "Haven't we trick-or-treated at every house on this street before? I don't remember her at all."

"We should report her. She shouldn't oughta be scaring kids with that death stuff," Nikki said.

"But, listen!" Elspeth said loudly, almost shouting. "She found that skull by the house. A dog skull. You and I heard a dog crying from there. Same dog, I'll bet. And I think I was right...it's a ghost dog. We should go in there and find it and try to help it."

"Nope," Nikki insisted. "I ain't goin' there. And that dog's head we saw poking out through the window...it must have been a different dog...a *real* dog. *Real* dogs can't be missing their skulls. And *real* dogs can bite. That lady was, like, a witch or something."

"Ah, she was just trying harder to be spooky than most grown-ups do...you know, to make it more scarier," Damon said. "It's *Halloween*, Nikki! I wish more grown-ups would do scary things on Halloween. That lady got all dressed like a witch or something and had that skull story to freak kids out. I mean, she bothered to do all that. Pretty cool. I thought it was fun. But she was right. We all die someday."

Chapter 11
Into the House

As they neared the corner to turn onto Beechum Street, Elspeth began to sweat, even though the air was quite cool. Two street lights in a row were not working, one of them flickering a little off and on, and the other one completely out. Their approach to the corner was therefore dark and surreal and forbidding. Elspeth turned on the flashlight she was carrying. Damon said, "It's really quiet all of a sudden. Listen...no traffic or kids or anything. Weird."

Out of the blue, Elspeth boldly asked him, "Are you okay? I mean, did something happen to you that made you stay out of school?"

"What do you mean? Nothing happened. I was just, well, I had a temperature. I felt like crap, that's all."

"You said in school yesterday that you weren't sick. And Patrick said..."

"*What* did Patrick say?" Damon asked, harshly.

"Um, nothing. He just thought you might have gotten hurt."

"Well, Patrick's full of it. I was sick. I told him that. I was kidding yesterday when I said I wasn't."

Elspeth knew this discussion was over, and, to change the subject, asked, "Will you go with me up to the house?"

"What, *now*? *Tonight*?"

Nikki intervened. "No, Elspeth...your dad just said..."

"Will you?" she repeated.

"Why do you want to go there in the dark?" Damon said. "I mean, we have only one flashlight. There's a gate we'd have to climb over. And there's probably no electricity in there. Are you talking about the dog you heard?"

"And *saw*. Yes."

"'Speth!" Nikki objected.

"You can wait for us here while we check it out, Nik. But you can't have the flashlight."

"If you go there, I'm going to tell your dad."

Damon said, "I dunno, Elspeth. The police are everywhere tonight. We'd be trespassing."

"Oh, come on, Damon! I need to find out about the dog. What can happen?"

"Well, let's see...about a million things."

"Okay, I'll go by myself. You guys can wait here for me. I'm not going to stay long. And, by the way, it was you who suggested I check out the place."

"In the *daytime*, yeah. But...okay, jeez, I'll go," Damon said, "but we're not going to stay for more than a couple of minutes."

"I'm telling," Nikki said. "I don't want anyone to think I had anything to do with this."

"Fine," Elspeth countered. "But stay here until we come back. Okay?"

"Well, yeah! I'm not going to, like, walk all the way home by myself!"

And so, Damon and Elspeth approached the doors of the black iron gate, and were prepared to scale them, leaving their candy bags in Nikki's care. But when Damon pressed on one of the doors, it simply swung open. "That's bizarre! Anyone could just walk right in here," Damon observed. "So now, *we* can, too." They closed the door and inched forward, keeping their feet just behind the oblong beam of the flashlight.

"We need to listen for the dog, so let's not talk."

"Wait." The two stopped abruptly, halfway along the walkway. "What are we going to do if there *is* a dog in there?" Damon asked.

"Let's just see if it's friendly. See if it will come with us..."

"Oh, great idea, Elspeth. So if it *isn't* friendly, we end up in pieces, scattered all over the house. Your dad just got through saying you couldn't go to the house, and he said it to *me*, so who's in trouble if something happens to us in there? I don't think you really have much of a plan."

The two stood quietly in place for a few minutes while Elspeth thought this through. Leaves were tumbling around on the ground, making the only clear noise they could hear. Until, that is, a dog began to bay from within the house, which was now only a few yards away.

Damon froze. "Holy...there really *is* a dog in there! You know what? I don't need to go in, really. Let's just call the animal rescue people and report it. Let *them* go in."

"Hey, I'm a girl with a fake leg, and I'm going inside, with you or without you."

"Okay...but if that thing in there isn't friendly, I'm hightailing it outta there."

"Agreed."

With her flashlight beam aimed alternately between the walkway and the front door of the house, Elspeth felt excited. Her heart was pounding furiously. Maybe she could rescue this poor, lonely animal!

Without surprise for either of them, the front door was locked. Above them, the sagging wooden canopy, still dripping from Monday's rain, was occupied by thick spider webs and small bird nests in its eves. The flooring of the porch felt spongy and unstable. The flashlight beam caught broken windows on both sides of the door, and the kids checked to see if they might be able to enter through one of them.

The window on the right was latched, but there were enough broken panes so that Damon could reach inside and unlock it. "I'll bet lots of kids have snuck into the house this way." After pushing the window up, he stuck his head through and heard nothing. Guided by Elspeth's flashlight, he climbed through the window, having to put his hands several feet down to reach the floor and using them to pull himself inside, as though he was the front of a wheelbarrow. "Stinks in here." Navigating shards of broken glass, he managed to avoid cutting himself. He brushed the floor with his feet, and helped Elspeth through. Not as lucky as Damon, she felt a sting a couple of times as her hands pressed down on tiny pieces of glass. Her prosthetic leg came down with a thud, and Damon helped her up.

They did not know where in the house they were. The walls were empty of hanging pictures, although lighter squares and rectangles were apparent from where they had once hung. The pale, patterned wallpaper was curling off in strips. Spider webs were everywhere, not just in corners. On the floor, there were droppings from mice or rats, and scattered rocks that had been thrown in from outside. The room smelled of mold.

They listened silently for a few moments, hearing nothing. But the house was large, so there would be many other rooms to check out.

"Elspeth, we oughta get out of here and forget about the dog, okay?"

"Well, we're already inside. But you know what?" Elspeth said, wiping her hands on her pants. "You could have opened the door and let me in that way."

"Ah, yes," Damon sneered, "thanks for thinking of that. Actually, *I* should have thought of that. Sorry."

"Hey! Help me in!" Nikki had suddenly appeared at the window. "I don't wanna be out here alone waiting for you guys."

Damon said, "How did you get all the way to the porch without a light?"

"I had to feel the sidewalk with my shoes. Come on...hurry up!"

"Wait at the door, and we'll let you in." Despite a Herculean effort, he was unable to throw back the deadbolt of the massive front door to let Nikki in. Instead, he found there was a side door at the bottom of the stairway in the hall, which he found easier to open. To the left and right of the door Nikki stepped in through was a pair of long, thick, stained glass windows, both of them a very deep red.

"This hallway must look pretty when it's sunny," Elspeth said. She shone the light over her head toward the high ceiling, and was delighted to see a chandelier with many dangling crystal prisms, and four hook-shaped brass holders for light bulbs, all of them missing. From the reflection of her light, the walls and doorway were suddenly dancing with rainbow-colored patterns. "This place is amazing!" Elspeth was feeling more relaxed now, and continued to try locating the dog she was sure lived there. "Hey, boy...come on...we're here to help you."

Nothing. No sounds other than those they were making.

"It's so dusty in here...I could catch asthma," Nikki complained. "Let's just walk out now and trick-or-treat on Beechum Street, okay? If we stay in here, we'll be late getting home." She then added, "You know, like, this is really dumb, 'cause I don't think the dog's even here now. It must have run outside."

But Elspeth was adamant. She convinced her friends to continue on into the house and, having no flashlights of their own, they followed.

The stairs were padded with worn-down carpeting, but were squeaky. The railing on their left wobbled as they guided themselves toward the second floor, feeling cobwebs stick to their skin. Elspeth continued to talk to the dog, in case one was even there, using her most maternal voice. Halfway up the staircase, the kids stopped dead in their tracks. They heard shuffling behind them, from the first floor. Something was walking down there. *Where they had just been*.

"Oh, God!" Nikki whispered. "We're dead! We can't get out now!"

"Shh!" Elspeth scolded. Then she said, "It's okay, boy..."

"How do you know it's a boy?" Nikki asked.

"It doesn't *know* what it is, so what difference does it make?" Damon said. "And, maybe it's not even a *dog*. Could be other kids in here trying to scare us. Quiet a minute. Just listen."

For several moments, there was the kind of silence one might experience if standing on a mountaintop with no wind or birds. Just an absolute, total, soundless vacuum.

Nikki said, "I'm not going up."

"Then just sit on the step and wait for us," Elspeth suggested.

"No, I don't wanna do that, either."

Damon, a bit fed up with her by now, said, "Look, Nikki, you're making this take too long. Let's just go to the top and look around really quick, and we'll leave, okay?"

Nikki murmured something and slowly took another step up. But then she stopped as she heard something upstairs ahead of them. "That was down *behind* us a minute ago...or maybe there's *two* of them!"

Elspeth called gently to the source of the noise again, hoping it would show itself, but also secretly afraid that it would.

"Okay," Damon said, "let's go back down. C'mon, *do* it, Elspeth. Turn your flashlight around and let's get outta here. We have to get you two home by eight."

Elspeth knew he was right, and turned around. Nikki, now having enough light to see forward, hurried down, even though she was afraid she might run into whatever had made the sound down there.

"Wait, Damon...I have to go down slowly because

of my..."

"Sure, okay," he said. He took Elspeth's flashlight in one hand while she held his arm, which helped her to maintain her balance down the eight steps they'd already climbed.

"Hey, Nikki! Wait up!" Damon called. Then he half-whispered, "Elspeth, do you *smell* that? What *is* that?" For just a second or two, the stairway smelled like old cabbage left much too long in the trash on a warm day.

The moment they reached the bottom, there was a sudden rush of damp, swirling air. "Whoa! What was that?" Elspeth called out for Nikki again and again. Nikki did not answer, and certainly wasn't in view within the beam of the flashlight as it moved back and forth. "Nik!" Not a stir from her friend. Or a dog. Or anything else.

"Elspeth, we've gotta leave! We can't wait..."

"Not until we find Nikki!" Moving ahead with great care, they hastily entered each room downstairs, aiming the light from corner to corner. "Oh, I am in *so...much...trouble*." Elspeth kept calling for her friend, with no response.

"We've got to leave *now*!"

"What? Leave Nikki by herself in here?"

Without warning, they were assaulted by a howling so loud it made them throw their hands up over their ears. Elspeth dropped her light. It went out.

Damon reached to grab it, as the roaring wail continued. He knocked the light against his wrist a few times until it blinked back on. "Come *on*!"

Elspeth was being pulled by Damon toward the side door, trying not to fall. "Nikki!" she cried again, over her shoulder. As she was being hustled along the hall, she heard the scampering of animal feet coming toward them from behind, its toenails skittering to grip the floor as it rounded a corner from another room. The two of them rushed outside through the door, shutting it firmly behind them.

Once they reached the gate, the first thing that stood out was that it was open. Pausing for breath, they looked back at the house, which was but a ghostly pale gray from the light of the rising half-moon. Elspeth suddenly began to sob. "Nikki! What if she's dead? What if...dammit, Damon, this is all my fault. Everything bad that happens is my fault. And...where are the candy bags? Damon, somebody stole our candy!"

"I guess we should tell the police...about the *dog*, I mean. Forget the candy!" Damon put his arm around Elspeth's shoulder. "I don't know what's in that house, but someone has to find out, and it ain't gonna be me. Or you. And we don't know where Nikki is, but she couldn't just disappear!" Damon began to cry, also, and the two hugged, feeling a tiny comfort through each other's convulsive shivers. This was too much to handle for a pair of ten-year-olds. Nikki was missing. *Now* what?

Walking along Beechum Street toward Elspeth's home, with Damon's arm still around her shoulder, she kept looking behind her, expecting Nikki to appear suddenly. To Damon, she said, "Thanks for helping me. I'm really sorry that all of this happened, and it's my fault. Oh, my god, *where is Nikki?*"

"She's right there! Look!" Damon shouted, aiming Elspeth's flashlight ahead on the sidewalk. Sure enough, Nikki was propped up against one of the trees that lined the street. Beside her was a single, half-full bag of candy.

"Is that you, 'Speth? Damon?"

The three of them group-hugged for several minutes, crying and laughing with gratitude that they'd all made it out of the house alive.

Catching her breath, Elspeth asked Nikki, "What *happened* to you in there?"

"I just heard something walking around really close to me as soon as I got downstairs, and I panicked and ran through the door and kept running until I got here. I thought we were all going to die in there. I didn't mean to leave you."

"Did you leave our candy back at the gate?"

"No. It wasn't there. I only have mine because I left it right outside the door where you let me in."

"So, somebody stole ours," Elspeth lamented. "Great! I don't know what I'm going to tell Mom and Dad about not having *my* candy."

"Hey, we're safe now. Forget the candy. Just make up an excuse," Damon said. "Hey, this has been some crazy Halloween, huh? C'mon, I'll walk you guys the rest of the way home."

Nikki broke off from the group first, as her home was a bit closer to the old house and school. "I'll see you later. Thanks, okay? I mean, it was an adventure for sure. Want some of my candy, 'Speth?"

"I guess not...I don't have anything to put it in."

Damon and Elspeth continued on past a few more houses. "What *are* you gonna tell your parents about losing all your candy?"

"Not sure. Maybe I'll just tell them the truth and

get in trouble, but at least Dad might call somebody to go to that house and see what's in there. You?"

"I don't care about the candy. I was going to give most of it to Freddie. My little brother."

Again, Elspeth pressed her friend, "Tell me the truth. Are you okay? I mean, is your dad..."

"He was drunk when I left tonight. He's always been a drunk. He gets really mean when he drinks. He hits my mom. Sometimes he hits me." Damon choked a little on his words, but was trying to sound blasé. He was, after all, telling this to a girl. "All right, look – I'll tell you something, but *only* you, okay? Last week he was drinking and he threw a fit because Mom said something he didn't like, and I told him to leave her alone. He shoved me against the refrigerator and punched me a couple of times. Mom kept me home from school because my stomach was really sore. He gave me that bruise on my face that you saw at lunch. When he doesn't drink, he's okay, almost like normal. But he doesn't get along with my mom most of the time and he keeps losing jobs and he just keeps drinking. I can't do anything about it..."

"Well, yes you *can*," Elspeth said. "You gotta *tell* somebody. They'll get help for you...and for him. And for your mom and your brother. You can't just keep getting beaten up."

"Look, it's better if you stay out of it. He's not always like that. I mean, if he gets a new job and he has some money, he won't drink as much. Just...well, you know, I really appreciate that you're worried about me, but you probably ought to just stay out of it, okay? I wish my brother and me could move in with another family. But, I'd miss my mom."

Elspeth knew she would not be able to stay out of it, hard as she might try.

In bed, following the Halloween fiasco, Elspeth tried to make sense of everything. She had seen skulls before – *human* ones – in movies and books and once in a museum. Placing her fingertips on her head, she explored the surface. Just beneath her scalp, which slid around a little as she massaged it, was the hardness of her own skull. She tried to imagine its shape without skin or hair. After feeling all around her cheeks and jaw, she touched her nose and ears knowing that, one day, after she'd been dead a little while, there would be only holes in their place. Her eyes would be gone, too. A dead person wouldn't need them, right?

With her right hand, Elspeth squeezed parts of her left hand, feeling the knuckles and connecting bones. In her arms, she could clearly detect two large bones, ending at the elbow. From there, a single, larger bone led to her shoulder. For the first time, she was truly cognizant of her ribs, and caressed their contours in her chest, wondering what they were for. Because her science classes had not explained any human anatomy to her yet, she made it a point to look for books about it at the library, so she would know better about the stuff that was inside of her. For now, though, the concept of her own death one day, and of being buried way under the ground forever, kept her awake for several hours.

Memento mori.

Chapter 12
Everything Changed

Elspeth dreaded the day after Halloween like no other day she'd had before. Standing at the curb for the school bus, feeling like she wanted to die, she was reliving her early morning. Her dad, on his way out the door to go to work, had told her she would not be allowed to see Damon after school anymore, and that he would be calling his parents. "Daddy! It wasn't his fault...it was *my* idea!"

"I told him not to let you go near the house, so it was as much his fault as yours."

"No, Daddy, *he tried to talk me out of it!* Please don't call his parents!"

"Elspeth, you are grounded for a month. No having Nikki over, no going to movies, no calling anyone on the phone, no..."

Elspeth was just sobbing and sobbing by now, but her dad was unwavering. It was a side of him she had never seen before, and it terrified her, even more than what had happened in the old house last night. Her mother, who had been watching all of this, simply kept quiet, her head down and her fingers over her mouth.

What could there possibly be in her life to look forward to now? Halloween had been a bust. She hadn't rescued the dog. Her dad had turned into a person she didn't recognize. She was grounded. School was going to be horrible. Plus, she was going to die one day. She was so deep into hopelessness she felt like running away...just letting her backpack slide to the curb and walking as fast as her prosthetic leg could take her, disappearing into a place where everyone loved her and she could be happy all the time.

There was, of course, no such place. Deep-down, she knew that.

Instead, she tried turning off all of her feelings about everything as she handed her backpack to the bus driver and pulled herself up the steps. Nobody made any wisecracks about her leg this morning as she headed up the aisle, for which she was grateful, but surprised. She sat on the outside this time, as it was Nikki's turn at the window. Neither girl spoke for a long while.

"Did you get in trouble?" Nikki asked, finally.

"Did you?" Elspeth countered.

"No, not really. I wasn't that late. You?"

"Oh, Nikki, I'm just..." Elspeth started to fall apart, but then took a deep breath and tried again. "My parents probably would have believed me if I'd said I didn't go in the house, and that somebody swiped the candy bag out of my hands and ran away, but then Mom noticed these," she said, turning her palms toward Nikki and showing her several tiny glass cuts. "So, I just told them what really happened. Then Dad went ballistic while Mom cleaned my hands, and sent me to bed and said we'd talk about it in the morning. That's what I get for telling the truth."

"And..."

"And, he...jeez, Nik, it's like he's someone *else's* dad now. Like maybe Damon's! Really mean and shouting at me. He grounded me. I can't even see you anymore except at school and on the bus. And I'm s'posed to stay away from Damon even at school!"

"Oh, 'Speth, I'm really sorry... Maybe this was partly my fault..." Nikki said, taking hold of and squeezing her friend's hand without thinking.

"Ow!" Elspeth said, pulling back.

"Sorry." Nikki reached into her backpack and pulled out a small paper bag, handing it to Elspeth. "Here."

"What is it?" She peered inside and sort of smiled.

"Some of the Halloween candy I got last night. I don't need it all."

"Thanks, Nik. But, you know what's the worst part? Dad's gonna call *Damon's* dad..."

"Oh, no! He can't! Oh, *no*!"

"I've gotta warn Damon at lunch."

"But, like, would that *help*?"

Damon was not at lunch.

Elspeth thought maybe she'd approach the boys' table in the back again to ask if they knew anything, but decided against it. She was feeling much too vulnerable just then, and didn't need sarcasm from any of Damon's pals.

"Aren't you going to eat?" Nikki asked, as Elspeth just stared across to where some of the fast eaters were returning their trays.

"No, aren't *you*?"

Nikki shoved her tray forward. "Nah. Not hungry."

"The lunch ladies are going to tell us we should eat

this, you know."

"I don't care. Anyway, I don't think they can really *force* us to eat, even if they say they can. I'll just go to the principal's office if I have to. I mean, they wouldn't expect us to eat dog food, so they shouldn't expect us to eat this moldy meat."

But the proctors allowed the kids to dump all the food they wouldn't eat and get in line without saying a word to them.

"Hmm...that's weird," Nikki whispered, before breaking from Elspeth to go to her room. "Hey, see you at recess."

At recess with all the third and fourth graders, Elspeth joined Nikki to stroll around in a square outlining the school yard. A boy approached and tapped her on the shoulder. "Elspeth?"

Spinning around, startled, she said, "What?"

"Come 'ere a minute. Gotta talk."

Elspeth recognized the boy. It was Patrick, from the table where Damon and his friends sat at lunch. "Just a minute, Nik...I'll be right back."

Patrick led Elspeth a distance away from anyone else, and said, "You heard, right?"

"Huh?"

"Oh, damn, you didn't hear. It was on the news this morning."

"What *is* it?"

"Well, Damon died."

Elspeth tried to process this, but failed. "No he didn't! He was trick-or-treating with us last night and..."

"No, he died *after* that. Like, way after midnight. I saw it from my bedroom window. An ambulance and some police cars were in front of his place, and they carried a stretcher out...the sheet was *covering his face*. He *died*, Elspeth."

Elspeth shook her head rapidly, trying to push out the information. "No..."

"Listen, I know you and Damon were really good friends. I gotta say, you have guts, Elspeth. I know you wanted to help him. None of the kids at my table will ever give you trouble again...I'll make sure of that. Sit with us tomorrow, and bring your friend."

Elspeth's head was a whirlwind of stuff she just couldn't handle right now. "*No...*"

"He was my friend, too. My *best* friend. I know this is all hard to believe. Hey, if you need to talk about him with anyone, I'll listen. Anytime. Okay?"

In an utter daze, Elspeth nodded silently. She'd heard what Patrick had said, but it was like he'd been in a cloudy dream of hers. Surely, she'd wake up soon and find out it wasn't even Halloween yet and that everything was normal.

"All right. I have to get ready to go inside. Just let me know if you need anything..."

Elspeth nodded again, in a daze. As Patrick left her, she dropped to her knees, and Nikki ran to her, squatting down and leaning her head against her friend's. "What is it, 'Speth?"

There were no words.

Chapter 13
...But Some Things Changed Back

While the kids in Elspeth's class waited for the bell at the end of the school day, the principal's voice came over the speakers mounted in every classroom. His voice sounded grave.

"Hello, students. Most of you have heard by now that we lost a very special friend of ours last night. Damon Clarke was a boy who liked everybody, and whom everybody liked..." The tears welled up in Elspeth's eyes again, as they did in the eyes of half the class. Mrs. Ewell was wiping hers dry with a handkerchief. "We're all going to feel the hurt from this for a long time. But, we'll pull through it, if we help each other by being thoughtful and kind.

"You might consider making a card for his parents. I have asked the teachers not to give you the usual homework for the rest of the week so that you could work on this. We'll make sure the Clarkes get it. Also, our nurses, Mrs. Langtoff and Miss Evans, will be available during the day tomorrow for you to talk to. Our hearts go out to Damon's family, and mine goes out to all of you. Please stay safe."

There was a click as the minute hand signaled the end of school, and the bell for dismissal filled the halls.

During the slow walk home, Nikki said, "The school knew about it, but they didn't tell us until it was time to go home. That doesn't seem right."

"Well, they probably thought nobody would learn anything if..."

"But, by recess, everybody knew about it anyway. They shoulda had, like, an assembly."

"Maybe. I don't know. Nik, it doesn't matter."

The two walked in silence for a few minutes until reaching the corner of Bax and Beechum Streets. There, they stopped. "I'll never go through *those* gates again!" Nikki sighed.

"I'd like to burn it down."

"It wasn't the house's fault about Damon..."

"I know...it was mine. I made him go..."

"*No,* 'Speth. He didn't *have* to go in there. He went in with you because you were his friend. *I* only went in because I was scared to stay *out*...you know, by myself. But Damon went in because he wanted to protect you. And he didn't die *there*. Right?"

"I still wish I could burn it down. Maybe I would, except..."

"Except for what? The *dog*? We don't even know for sure that..."

"Come on. I don't want to stand here anymore."

Hearing no sound coming from the house, the girls continued on toward home.

"How do you feel, 'Speth?"

"Like I want to cry and scream *all the time*. And I'm scared about when Dad gets home. Can you think of the worst day you could ever possibly have in your whole life?"

"Maybe if I thought about it..."

"Well, for me, this one is a thousand times worse."

"Yeah. I wish we could meet somewhere in secret and just talk for a long time."

"Can't, though. I'm..." and both girls, like twins might, sighed "grounded" at the same time. "Nik...has anyone in school said *how* Damon died?"

"Um...no. I didn't hear anything."

"I didn't either. What if his dad *did* kill him? We should tell somebody what we know."

"I think you should wait. I mean, let it die down for a while. You can't help Damon now, anyway."

"But, Nik...what about his younger brother?"

"Oh, yeah. I forgot. Let's talk about it at recess tomorrow...I've gotta go." Nikki turned into her driveway with a backwards wave.

Elspeth continued on past two more homes until reaching her own. She stopped at the head of her driveway and pivoted slowly around, looking at the neighborhood. The naked trees. The gray-pink clouds. The traffic. The cozy homes. A few song birds still warbled here and there and a cat that wasn't Lucie meowed down the street. A truck backed up somewhere and its warning beeps sounded. It still smelled a bit like Halloween. She began sniffling, because all of these sights and sounds and smells were ones her friend Damon would never enjoy again. And one day, neither would she.

She opened the door into her kitchen and walked into the outstretched arms of her mother, who held her tightly and stroked her hair. "Oh, sweetheart, I'm so sorry about your friend..."

"It's okay, Mom...well, *no*! It's *not* okay!" Elspeth finally caved in to her grief and let loose within her mother's nurturing embrace. She wept for a full five minutes, while Mom cradled her from side to side until she was able to speak again. "I don't think I can stand it, Mommy. It *sucks*! It's not *fair*!"

"No, it certainly *is not* fair. But I'm here. I'll help. Your father will help..."

"I don't think he'll help," Elspeth said, pulling her head back so that she could look up at Mom, her cheeks wet and her nose freely running. "I think he hates me now."

"Elspeth, come to the living room couch with me and let's talk about that, okay?"

The two sat on the couch, and Elspeth collapsed sideways so that her head rested on her mother's lap. "I'm going to tell you a few things about your father, and I want you to pay close attention. Can you do that?" Elspeth nodded. "He wouldn't approve of my telling you this, so it's between you and me. Daddy hasn't sold any houses for a couple months, and that's making him very nervous, because he counts on what he earns to provide for us. He's made a lot of sacrifices since we were married, and especially after we had you, to make sure he could give us the best life he could."

"Yeah...I know..."

"Well, he's worried. We have savings for a while, but also we have the house mortgage and...well, things will get better for him, because he's a terrific real estate broker. He's just having a bad luck streak. They all do. He knows that this is temporary, but it still puts him on edge, and it leaves him anxious when he gets home from work. He doesn't mean to treat us differently, but little things set him off. Do you understand?"

"I guess. But, Mom...what about when you were arguing two nights ago?"

"You heard that?"

"Yes, I did," she asserted. "I'm worried you two will get divorced..."

"No, sweetie. We aren't that fragile," Mom said, stroking Elspeth's hair, which usually comforted her. "I'm sure it sounded scary to you, but..."

"Mom, he thinks he was the one who caused me to lose my leg, but he takes it out on *me*."

"Of *course* he's always felt responsible for the accident..."

"I'd rather eat supper now and be in my room when Daddy gets home."

"Oh, Elspeth, that would *not* be acceptable. We're a family, and we have to work things out *as* a family. Can't hide, little one. We'll all eat together."

Dad arrived home at the usual time, winked at Mom, smiled broadly at Elspeth, and said, "Hey, Little Squirrel...where's my hug?"

Instantly brimming with relief and love, as though her face had been erased and a brand new one had just grown there, she ran to him, jumped up, wrapped her legs around his waist, and proceeded to loosen his tie.

Elspeth felt that a horrible weight had been lifted from her shoulders. After all, if her parents were okay, then all was well with the world.

Well, no, not *all*. The card. She had to write a card to the Clarkes.

Completing this assignment seemed impossible. It wasn't just about trying to punctuate a sentence. This was about writing a card of condolence to the parents of her dead friend. That meant it would be read by his dad as well as his mom. How was she supposed to do this after what Patrick had told her at school and after what Damon had told her on Halloween? She now knew, and probably other kids knew, that Damon's father was cruel when he drank too much. But, most times, everyone seemed to think he was a real nice guy who went to church every week, and who volunteered as a coach for his son's Little League, and who helped his elderly neighbors paint their shutters or drive them to the supermarket.

And the news had said nothing about Damon dying from any sort of injury. They only said he had died "unexpectedly." Wasn't anyone else wondering why or how?

The card, she decided, could wait.

After brushing her teeth and hopping into bed, both her parents came to her room to tuck her in, which hadn't happened the past few nights. Mom kissed her forehead sweetly, and Dad lightened the mood by telling her a few jokes and tickling her until she breathlessly told him to stop.

She felt strengthened. Emboldened. Ready to help Damon, even though he was gone now.

Chapter 14
The Air Was Thick on Friday

The hallways, the lunchroom, even the recess yard, were restrained on Friday morning.

Conversations that were generally lively – so loud you could barely hear one voice over the next – were, instead, mere whispers. Yet, there was an urgency to them. It was more in the tone than in the volume of the students' talk that day that suggested something was in the air that went beyond mere grief. Indeed, out of earshot of the teachers, kids throughout the older grades were sharing their theories about what had happened to Damon.

At lunch, Patrick reminded Elspeth and Nikki that they were invited to sit at the boys' table at the back of the cafeteria, so they carried their trays across the room, quite aware that this was a privilege. Patrick seemed to be the spokesperson, and more or less initiated a meeting. "Hey, guys...I invited the girls here because they were good friends of Damon's. He talked about them with us sometimes. I trust them."

One of the other boys at the table said, "Hi, Elspeth." He glanced at Nikki. "I don't know who *you* are..."

"You can just call me 'Nik.'"

"And I'm just 'Speth. It's easier."

"Where did you get your name, 'Speth?" one of

boys asked.

"Well, Dad loves this movie called *Dragonslayer*. The princess in that is called Elspeth. He liked the name and gave it to me."

"How cool! I love that movie!"

Patrick got the conversation back on track. "Can either of you tell us what happened on Halloween?"

Elspeth said. "I think he was killed."

"How come you think that?" asked another boy.

"He told me on Halloween night about his father drinking and getting mean and hitting his mom and him. Maybe he was late getting home after he trick-or-treated with us and his dad got mad. That's my fault. I talked him into going into the old house with me..."

"*You* went *into* the house?" somebody asked.

The boys looked at each other like she'd just told them they'd been to Mars and back.

"Nobody goes in that place, especially at night!"

Nikki, feeling a bit left out, said, "All *three* of us did."

"The news didn't ever say how Damon died."

"Yeah," another boy piped in, "they just said it was such a shame, because he was so young, and it was unexpected, and all that."

"I just think we have to tell the police about what he said to me, and about what he told you, Patrick," Elspeth said, bluntly.

For a minute, everyone ate bites of their macaroni and cheese and hot dogs, thinking over what she'd suggested. "I met Mr. Clarke a lot of times," Patrick said. "He seemed pretty cool. I mean, he didn't...he wasn't drunk or anything. He took Damon places sometimes and bought him a bike when it wasn't even his birthday and stuff. When he told me about his dad drinking and hitting his mom, I couldn't really imagine it, you know? But, he did kill Damon's dog last year."

Elspeth leaned forward. "Huh?"

"Damon and Freddie had a pet dog. It snarled at Mr. Clarke when he threatened to hit Damon, so Mr. Clarke picked up a kitchen chair and broke it over the dog's head. Then he took it out and buried it where the old house is. I know, because Damon called me every day. That's how I found out he was beaten up. But one day his dad caught Damon talking to me, and he grabbed the phone out of his hands and hung up on me. That was the last time Damon called me, ever. We just had to see each other at lunch and on the playground. And then, he didn't talk about it much."

"You should've called the police right then, Patrick," one of his friends said.

Patrick was a dark-haired, dark-eyed boy whose face was very intense when he was in a certain mood, but most times was open and warm and full of laughter. Today at lunch, it was intense. There were deep wrinkles between his eyes and his brow was lowered. His stare was piercing, like a laser beam. "All I know is that this makes me so mad I want to scream, or..."

"Well," Elspeth began, wanting to fit into this new social circle, "why don't we do what we're supposed to do for homework, and write a letter to Mr. and Mrs. Clarke."

"Huh? We don't want to send a letter to *him*..."

"But we don't know for sure that *he* made Damon

die. And Mrs. Clarke must be feeling just awful. We should send a card from anybody who wants to sign it."

Nikki was confused by her friend's idea, and said so. "I don't get it, 'Speth. How do you think that would do any good? What are we going to say in the card?"

"Well, let's talk about that," Elspeth said, and for the remainder of their short lunch period, between mouthfuls of a school meal they actually liked, they discussed how to word a card they could send to the Clarke home.

By the end of the school day, a card with a message written by Elspeth, and added to a bit by Nikki and some of the boys, had been carried around among third and fourth graders during afternoon recess, many of whom signed it. But Elspeth didn't feel right about turning it in for the school to deliver without first getting one more opinion...

Her dad's.

Chapter 15
The Card

Dad was in his office at home, working on real estate business. "Hi, Little Squirrel. Come on in."

"Hi, Daddy," she said, sitting in the chair beside him, and balancing the open card atop his cluttered desk.

"What's this?"

"Could you read it, please?"

Dad took the card and held it under his desk lamp, adjusting his glasses a bit. He recited out loud what Elspeth had written, stumbling over her handwriting a few times. "'Dear Mr. and Mrs. Clarke...' Who are Mr. and Mrs. Clarke, Elspeth?"

"They're Damon's mom and dad."

"You mean...oh, the boy who..."

"Yeah."

Dad continued reading, more intently now.

"'We are all very sad about Damon. We feel very bad for you because he was a nice boy and everybody at school liked him. He talked to us about a lot of things at school, like about when he got hurt and missed a few days and had bruises. None of us knows what happened to make him die. We think maybe he got hurt on his way home from Halloween.'"

"Is that okay?"

"Honey," Dad said, looking up at his daughter, who was studying his face for a reaction, "this is...what are you trying to say in this letter? It's obvious you kids are all trying to help, but I don't think that the Clarkes would appreciate..."

"Daddy, please just read the end."

Dad sighed through his nose and tilted his head back toward the card.

"'We want to talk to the police because Damon was with us when we were trick-or-treating, and we all went into that old house on the corner. He said some things about being upset at home, and after that he walked home by himself. We were worried about him. Anyway, we hope you are okay. Yours truly, the kids in third and fourth grade.'"

There were about thirty small signatures all over the card on the inside and on the back.

"Is it good?"

Dad handed the card back across the desk. "I don't know what to say. You aren't planning on actually sending this, are you?"

"Yeah, of course! But I wanted to show it to you first."

"But you're...this sounds like you're suggesting... I really don't know what you're trying to do here, but I would strongly encourage you to bring that to your teacher and work on it some more. You want to make the Clarkes feel *better*, not worse, right?"

"Mmm...well, *Mrs*. Clarke, at least."

"What do you mean? Not *Mr*. Clarke?"

"Daddy, most of my class think that he hurt Damon and probably killed him. Not on purpose. Accidentally, because he was drunk..."

"Whoa! Wait a minute, there, kid..."

"There's a boy at school named Patrick who lives next to Damon's house and they were best friends, and Damon told him that he was beaten up a few times by his dad. Mrs. Clarke was beaten up, too. Damon was out of school for three days."

"Oh, sweetheart, you're taking the word of a boy living next door to him?"

"Not only that...Damon told *me*, too."

"When?"

"When he was walking me home from trick-or-treating. He was being abused, Dad!"

Daddy sat thoughtfully for a moment while Elspeth watched him with worshipful eyes, hoping for a little support.

"No," he said, gently, "this really isn't the way to handle it."

"I was going to make a copy and send one to the police."

"Come on up here, Little Squirrel." Elspeth positioned herself on her father's lap, and he spoke very quietly into her ear. "I am very proud of you."

"You are?"

"Obviously, you were an awfully good friend to Damon."

"Yeah. I wish you got to know him, Dad."

"You are brave and thoughtful to do this, and it shows what a good heart you have. But I don't think this is the best way to help Damon out now. Besides," he added, giving her a wink, "it's too long, and you misspelled 'bruise.'"

Elspeth looked a bit dejected. "But I gotta do something! I only have 'til Monday."

"Here's what we can do...but I'll need your approval."

"What?"

"I will call the police and ask if they can send somebody over to listen to your story. It's better if we let them handle this. Think about the kind of trouble you might be stirring up if this Mr. Clarke is as bad as you say he is. After all, he would have all your names on that card."

Elspeth had not thought of it that way, and she shivered. "Mmm...yeah...I guess so. But we have to do something pretty fast, because there's another boy in the house...younger than Damon. I think he's in preschool or something."

"I'm going to get right on it. First thing in the morning, I'll call Detective Todd...he was a client of mine. In fact, I sold him his house."

"I still want to send *Mrs.* Clarke a card..."

"I don't see how you can send one to her and not to him, do you?"

"No, I guess not. But now I'll have to make another card and get the kids to sign it again."

"We can work on that together. You want to? Right now?"

Elspeth threw her arms around her father's neck. "I love you, Daddy."

"I love you, too, Little Squirrel, but not so tight...I can't breathe!" he said, pretending to choke, which made Elspeth giggle. What a relief to laugh!

After about a half-hour, she headed up to bed holding a newly-written card, secure in the belief that everything was going to be all right now. After she'd been tucked in and the light was out, something continued to nag at her: that dog in the house.

There really *was* a dog in there, wasn't there? Maybe a real dog, maybe a ghost dog. All three kids had heard it, and she and Nikki had *seen* it. Probably, Elspeth fancied, it was feeling lonely and lost, and the kids had just frightened it and caused it to come after them in the hallway. Or was that even a dog in there? What if it wasn't a sad, lonely dog at all...what if it was an angry, horrible monster animal that would have devoured them had it caught them before they got out the door? So, why had Elspeth been on a crusade to rescue an animal she knew nothing about, an animal that maybe didn't want to be rescued at all, but wanted to be left alone. What if...what if?...what if...?

What was the truth behind whatever was haunting the house on the corner of Bax and Beechum Streets?

Chapter 16
Peccadillos

It was not only raining, moderately, as Elspeth was driven to school the following Monday morning – picking up Nikki on the way – it was also nearly cold enough to be snowing. The girls were both wearing raincoats (one red, one yellow) and matching hats, and the back seat where they were buckled in was wet from their dripping.

"Did you bring the card we signed?" Nikki asked.

"It's in my backpack." Elspeth did not volunteer to her friend that her dad had helped her completely rewrite it.

There was no outdoor recess to look forward to again today, which was a bummer. And this was only Monday. Not good. But there'd be tacos for lunch. Check. Mrs. Ewell would probably show a movie, as she did on some rainy days. Check. She decided she could survive this.

Elspeth took the new card around, which most of the kids did not even bother to read this time before adding a signature, and handed it to Mrs. Ewell, who read it and smiled with approval. "Nice work, Elspeth."

Detective Todd knocked on the Amesbury' front door at a little past four that day. Elspeth's mom took his coat and hat, and showed him to a chair, offering coffee. He said, "Hello, young lady – Elspeth, is it? Are you the brave one who went into the house on the corner? On Halloween night?"

"Yes, sir," she said. "My friends Nikki and Damon were with me."

"Your father tells me that you were instructed not to go in there. Is that right?"

Elspeth was twitching in her chair a bit. "Yes, sir."

"Do you think it was a good idea for you to go in there anyway?"

"No, sir. But that isn't..."

"You have some information about your classmate who died on Tuesday night, right?"

"He wasn't in my class. I mean, he was in fourth grade, but not my class."

"Okay..."

Elspeth began glancing all over the room as though she'd never seen it before, trying to avoid eye contact with the detective as his tone grew more serious. But then, she decided to confront the problem face-on, and looked directly at the man. "Most of the kids in my class think that Mr. Clarke killed Damon."

"All right...I was getting to that. Why do you think he might have?"

And for almost an hour, Elspeth answered more questions and became more confident that what she was telling Detective Todd was going to help with the investigation. She repeated almost word-for-word what Damon had told her Halloween night.

"Well, okay, Elspeth," the man said. "You did some things that were wrong, but I think you did them for good reasons. So, we'll chalk all that up to peccadillos. I'm sure that if a dog is really in that house..." He then saw that Elspeth was giving him a look of great worry. "Tell you what, I'll ask a couple of officers to check it out. If they find a dog in there, we'll have animal control bring it to the shelter. Okay?"

"Okay. Thank you."

"No, thank *you* for your help...I'm sure Damon would thank you if he could. And thank you for the coffee, Mrs. Amesbury."

"Sally."

"Okay, Sally. Thank you for the coffee. I'm Renner," he said, picking up his hat and coat. "I'll be off now to talk to Patrick. You all have a great day."

"Say 'Hi' to Patrick for me."

"Okay, Elspeth. I will, I promise." And with that, Detective Todd was out the door.

"Mommy...if they find the dog and bring it to a shelter, can we adopt it? Pl-e-eze?"

"Sweetie, we don't know anything about the dog, or if there even is one..."

"There *is* one!"

"Okay, let's say there is one. If it's a wild dog, it could be dangerous. It could have rabies."

"But, if it isn't dangerous and it doesn't got ra..."

"Doesn't *have*..."

"If it doesn't *have* rabies, can we adopt it?"

"I know you hate to hear us say this all the time, but...we'll see."

Abruptly changing the subject, Elspeth asked, "Can Nikki and I go to the movies tomorrow?"

"Well..."

And both Elspeth and her mother said, "We'll see"

at exactly the same time.

Then Elspeth remembered that the matinee this week was about the Baskervilles hound dog.

"Um, no, instead of going to a movie, can she just come over?"

"That would be all right with me, as long as..."

"Nikki's mom will say yes."

"You should go to her house more often," Mom suggested, as she took ingredients for tuna casserole out of the cupboards. The second she placed two cans of tuna on the counter, Lucie appeared out of nowhere, rubbing against Mom's ankles with a meow. "I'll never figure out how that cat learned how to read the label on a can," she said.

"Come 'ere, Lucie," Elspeth said, picking the cat up to keep her from being an annoyance.

"What did you think of Detective Todd?"

"Oh, he was nice. Is that the one Daddy knows?"

"Yes. He bought a house..."

"I remember."

"Did it make you nervous to answer his questions?"

"Well, a little at first. But it was easy after that. Mom? Do you think I did okay? I mean, do you think it will help?"

"Oh, I am sure of it. You did well, sweetie. Daddy will be proud of you."

And he was.

Elspeth's world seemed mixed-up right now, and she wasn't yet sure whether it had gotten better, or was about to get a whole lot worse.

Chapter 17
Process

Elspeth started to feel a terrible fear welling up inside her.

It was after two in the morning according to her bedside clock, and she hadn't slept yet. No matter how much she turned over on her right side, then her back, then her left side, then her stomach, she could not find a comfortable position. She got up to pee even though she didn't need to, and while in the hallway stared at the dim outline of her parents' bedroom door, wondering if she should wake them and tell them about her anxiety, but then thought the better of it. She'd already awakened them once while Nikki was sleeping over. Dad would be mad.

Returning to bed, she turned on her little bedside light, its transparent lampshade revealing a repeating pattern of lambs jumping over a brick wall. Trying to read herself to sleep, she wasn't able to understand what the pages said. No sentences made sense. She had to read every line five or six times before it even began to seem like English rather than gibberish.

Damon's death was eating away at her as might a shark that caught her swimming in the ocean. Damon was the first person she'd known personally, of her own age, who had died. Actually *died*. She'd seen young kids die in movies and on TV, but this was different. Whispering out loud, for the benefit of her rabbit Jumper, of course, she said, "If ten-year-old kids can die...that means that *I* can die. All of a sudden, I could just stop living here or anywhere anymore...*forever*. What will Mom and Dad do? I guess they'd feel terrible for a while, but then they'd just go back to being normal and not think about me anymore. They'll put more pictures of me in little frames around the house, but after a while, they won't really look at them except when Mom is dusting. Right, Jumper? And where will I be? Will I be in Heaven?"

She put down her book, but left the bedside lamp on, fluffing up her pillow and continuing to toss and turn, not able to imagine a world that didn't have her in it. Her fears about death were stronger by a mile now than any she might have had after the car accident, but she began to think about that also: I could have died right then in the car when I was just six years old, and Mommy, too. *Anyone can die any time*, for no good reason! What if Daddy *did* cause the accident? No. No way.

She studied her room. The bookshelf was still partly cleared off for the Halloween candy that never found its way there. Beside it was her roll-up desk, given to her by her grandmother for her to use for when homework started getting heavier. A cork bulletin board hung on the wall beside her closet door, pocked with push-pins holding up drawings she had made of Lucie, a few small photos of her favorite rock stars she'd cut out of magazines, and some postcards people had sent her. These are *my* things, she thought. They can't be without me. Lucie can't.

Jumper can't. No way somebody my age should die. Even old people shouldn't die, like Grandmama. Nobody should die, except bad people. It's not fair! Most people should live forever!

But Damon had died. He wasn't bad. He didn't deserve to be dead when he was ten. She had just been talking with him on Halloween night. Now, Elspeth contemplated, I'll never talk to him again, ever. If I die, nobody could talk to me, either. And I couldn't talk to them. No, this isn't right!

She prayed that Damon would be okay, and that he would be safe, and wondered if he was in Heaven. Finally, she drifted off into an uneasy sleep, only to wake up to the knock of her mom at the door, telling her it was time to get up for breakfast and school. Her bedside light was still on. She had forgotten to set her alarm.

It was an effort to get herself dressed and downstairs for breakfast. Dad, as usual, had already left for work, and Mom was busy frying a couple of eggs to go with her two slices of bacon. She put the plate in front of Elspeth and returned to the sink to soak the pan. Elspeth got up from the table and walked quickly to the downstairs bathroom, afraid she was going to vomit. There was no appetite for breakfast, only a terrible, nervous nausea.

"Elspeth? Are you sick?"

After taking many deep breaths, she recovered enough to be able to return to the table, just as Lucie dragged a piece of bacon off her plate and down onto the floor, where she began choking it down. "Lucie! Bad cat!" Elspeth scolded. Lucie looked at her with no fear whatsoever, and continued to toss her head back, swallowing more bits of bacon.

Elspeth, as though suddenly possessed, kicked at her cat, which sent the startled animal scurrying away down the steps to the recreation room, still holding a half-piece of bacon in her jaws. "I *hate* you!" she yelled.

Mom put her hands on Elspeth's shoulders from behind. "Want to talk about it?"

"No!" she growled.

Mom sensed a rebellion in progress. She could just let it go, and eventually Elspeth would calm down, but she did not want her daughter going to school this way, and forcibly spun her around so that they were face to face. "Now, listen here...you're my daughter and I love you, but we need to be more honest with each other. I know it's almost time for the bus, but how about we just sit and talk for a while, and I'll drive you to school later with a note for Mrs. Ewell."

Elspeth considered this offer and decided she really needed to calm herself before she went back to school. "O-*kay*."

"What can you tell me about what just happened? Just now, with Lucie, I mean."

"I don't know..." Without meeting her mother's eyes, she asked, "I'm gonna die, right?"

"What on Earth made you think...?"

"Come on, Mom!" Elspeth demanded, now looking at her mother directly. "I am gonna die, right?"

"Well...*one* day, like everybody does...but not for a long, long time..."

"Why? 'Cause I'm only ten years old?"

"Well...yes..."

"*So was Damon.*"

"Sweetie, Damon lived in a house with a father who was sometimes very violent. You live in a house where your parents both love you and..."

"Not *all* the time. Daddy doesn't love me *all* the time."

"Well, now, that's silly," Mom said. "Daddy loves you every minute of every day. He just gets angry sometimes, like *you* do. Right? Like you are right *now*."

"If Daddy *always* loves me..."

"Yes, you were going to say...?"

"I wouldn't have a fake leg." Elspeth thought: There, I *said* it.

"Oh, now, sweetie..."

"And kids wouldn't make fun of me. And he would listen to me when I tell things like when I told him about the dog in the house, instead of calling me a liar."

"Your daddy never called you a liar."

"I'm going to school. See ya," Elspeth stated, flatly, and went through the door just as the bus was pulling up to the curb.

Behind her, Mom was running out calling her name, holding out her backpack.

The folding door opened, and Mom handed the driver the backpack, while her daughter, without looking back, grabbed the bar and climbed up the steps, heading to the back of the bus, where Nikki sat waiting.

She watched her mother through the window as the bus pulled away. She looked sad and frustrated as she waved Elspeth goodbye.

Elspeth did not wave back, but felt that awful

despair engulfing her again.

This was going to be a terrible day.

Again.

School was just not the same. Nikki and Elspeth, choosing to sit at their usual lunch table even though they had an invitation to sit with the boys, found laughter hard to come by. Things like math and grammar and history were almost impossible to absorb, and Elspeth did poorly on a quiz, which for her was like forgetting to wear her prosthesis to school. The weather didn't help. It was cold enough now so on days such as this one, kids had to don mittens and heavier coats.

Elspeth thought that, maybe, she should ask for a pass from Mrs. Ewell to visit one of the school doctors who were helping kids deal with Damon's death. No one else in her class had done that, so she decided not to. But she needed emotional closeness and support from *someone*, she just wasn't sure who. Nikki? Well, up to a point, Nik would be in her corner, but was also a little timid and even contrary sometimes. Mom and Dad? Sometimes, depending upon Dad's mood. Patrick? She didn't know him well enough to be able to count on him. Lucie? Jumper?

And so, Elspeth's day passed with nothing being resolved.

Chapter 18
Visitor

The following night, Mom and Dad both tucked her in together, and she hoped this would become a routine now. It so helped her to fall off to sleep, knowing that both her parents loved her and each other, and that their caring faces would be the last things she would see before her bedroom light went off. As usual, her door was left open a sliver for Lucie.

She wasn't sure whether or not she'd been asleep for a while before she found herself staring at the very dim crack at her door. There was a mere modicum of dull gray sneaking in, probably from the downstairs security light. Her own bedroom night light wasn't on because the tiny bulb had blown a few days ago. The digital clock on her bedside table emitted only a feeble green light, which did not penetrate the darkness more than an inch or two. There was no sound from anywhere in the house, meaning that her parents were in their room and sleeping at the end of the hall.

Her window was open just an inch, allowing a dab of fresh air inside, and making it possible for her to hear that the rain had stopped, but the wind had picked up. When a small gust of it blew into her face, it smelled like lilacs – her favorite smell ever – which was weird, because lilacs only bloomed briefly in the spring.

She heard Lucie downstairs. Hissing.

Then she heard what sounded like something with long toenails crossing the kitchen floor, click-click-click. Elspeth pulled her blankets up to her chin, now fully alert. She started to reach for her bedside lamp, but pulled her hand back when she heard a deep snort. Her heart was pounding furiously, and for a moment she thought maybe she'd turn her light on and rush out to her parents' bedroom. But she did not want to reveal where she was. In fact, she didn't dare to move. Something was starting up the stairs... something heavy. Something large.

Elspeth grabbed Jumper, and squeezed him tightly. The padding of the feet could now be heard in the hallway, just down from her room. Then, there was a long period of dead silence from outside her door. She could only hear tree branches rattling in her yard from the occasional breeze. There was no moon to provide any additional light. Elspeth was drowning in blackness.

Then, she heard sniffing. It wasn't loud, and in fact was barely perceptible, but she heard it, all right. Something was finding its way along the hallway carpet, following the scent left there by...her.

Elspeth's throat was tightening from panic. If she as much as coughed or even shuffled her blanket, it would be heard out in the hall by sensitive ears. Again, there was silence. What if she were to sneak very carefully out of her bed, tip-toe to her door to close and lock it, and then yell for her mom and dad? Tip-toe? With a crutch? No, she had to be completely still until, hopefully the...

Then Elspeth thought with panic, *It's that dog*! It must have followed her scent all the way from the corner of Bax and Beechum, and somehow managed to get inside her house. She realized, too late, that she'd been wrong...this was no friendly, pathetic mutt awaiting rescue. No, it was a devil dog that had come to punish her for trespassing in its domain.

She held her breath, listening intently. No sound, as though all air had been sucked from the hallway and from her bedroom. She was so close to letting out a scream that she bit her lip trying to hold it in. If she screamed, she'd be dead, like Damon. Sweat was beginning to seep from her forehead. She felt goose bumps growing like mushrooms from her arms. Her saliva tasted sour, like it did just before throwing up.

There was more sniffing, louder now, and therefore closer to her room. Then, as she stared at the barely-perceived crack at the door, she could see it widening, ever so slowly, and without a sound. Her lips were trembling, forming the word "Daddy," but not speaking it.

The bedroom door was now open wide enough for something really big to slip inside.

Again, there was a long period of silence, followed by another round of sniffing, which continued to approach her more closely, until it was right beside her bed. Elspeth was sure she would die of fear. A ten-year-old heart attack. And no one would ever know why.

Something warm was hitting her face now, at intervals. She could hear it panting. She was feeling the creature's breath, and it smelled like dirt and mold, but also a little bit like lilacs. She squeezed her eyes shut, expecting to be bitten over and over again, her throat gutted and ligaments pulled out, until she was just a bloody dead heap on the bed. Her parents would find her and wish they had done something about it when Elspeth had first told them about the dog.

To her further horror, something hot and wet began running up along her right cheek, over and over. She heard herself groan out loud and, in that instant, the breath against her face pulled back, and Elspeth saw the bedroom door give a little more as whatever had been beside her moved back into the hall.

Elspeth thought: it's going to go into Mom's and Dad's room... But, no, her parents always kept their bedroom door completely closed. Still, it got into the house, so it must be able to go right through things like walls and doors, right? A ghost dog.

Then, the muffled padding of animal footsteps receded from the hall, and she could hear it traveling down the stairs. Lucie hissed again, followed by silence.

Elspeth didn't move for many minutes. When she was fairly certain that the dog, or whatever it was, had left her house, she reached under the bed, grabbed her crutch, and hurried from her room to her parents' door, screaming. When it opened, Elspeth flew into her father's arms, sobbing into his pajama shirt and telling him that something horrible had just been in her room. She slept between her mom and dad for the rest of the night, until awakened by Mom getting up to fix breakfast. There was a pool of drool on her pillow, and she wiped her mouth as she sat up on the bed.

The smell of pancake batter made her stomach rumble. Still shaking from the events of last night, she steeled herself, returned to her bedroom to put on her prosthesis, and headed downstairs to the kitchen. "Can I help make those?"

"Sure. Can you reach?" Mom asked.

Elspeth took the spatula and stood up close to the stove. "Yup."

"When you see the bottoms of those start to brown around the edges, flip them over. They don't take long, so keep an eye out."

Dad wandered in, yawning, wearing his robe. "Had to get up when I smelled that!" he said. "Oh, a second pair of hands this morning."

Elspeth smiled and continued watching the pancakes vigilantly.

"Little Squirrel, you must have had a really bad nightmare last night."

"It wasn't a dream."

"You're saying a dog came into your room...how could it get into the house, first of all?"

"I don't know."

"Well, are you thinking it's that same dog you were looking for on Halloween?"

"I think so. And I don't think it's friendly. I think it's mad at me."

"Honey," Mom said, "She's had a scare and we should just let her do the pancakes. Otherwise, we're going to be eating charcoal patties."

Elspeth tried flipping the cakes, and got two of them right, but the third fell apart. "I'll eat that one," she said. "It'll taste the same."

"That's fine, honey. As soon as you put those on the serving plate, I'll pour three more."

"Mom?"

"Hmm?"

"I don't wanna sleep in my room anymore."

Dad piped in. "Now, wait a minute. It was a bad dream. We haven't any other room to put you in, anyway."

"I could just stay in your room. Maybe use a cot."

"No," Dad began, before Mom cut him off.

"Ray, let's just leave it for now. We'll figure it out later."

Elspeth was thinking: Now I've done it. They're gonna argue again. About me.

Breakfast ended precariously, but at least nobody started shouting, which was what Elspeth hated most.

However, she was back to thinking that no one was going to believe her. Not Dad, not Mom, not Detective Todd. Only Nikki and Patrick. And Damon, if he hadn't died.

Chapter 19
The Same Much

Saturday was like having a day off from fear and misery. The weather had reversed itself and provided plenty of sun and sixty-eight degrees. Houseflies suddenly became abundant again. People were walking their dogs along the sidewalks without even wearing sweaters. Birds might have wondered if flying south was even necessary. About the only things that betrayed the illusion of a second summer were the naked branches of every deciduous tree in sight, and the enticing fragrance of burning leaves.

It was a day for exploring. Elspeth called Nikki and asked her if she wanted to walk up Beechum Street and then on to Bax Street, and maybe keep on going past the school to get a look at Damon's house. Mom told her it would be okay for the girls to walk, but only as far as the school, not to the Clarke house.

She did not follow those instructions. It was just too nice a day, and Elspeth was simply driven to see where Damon had lived. They met at the curb, both wearing short-sleeve shirts and Nikki wearing cut-off shorts, and struck out on their afternoon adventure.

Most of the fallen leaves had been cleared from the sidewalks. It was still morning by a little, and the shadows cast by the girls were shortening as the minutes hurried by. Colors were especially vivid that day, which largely compensated for the lack of foliage. Houses painted red or blue and their bright shutters jumped out like headlights in the dark. The cloudless sky resembled a dome made of deep, tropical seawater.

Reaching the house on the corner, the girls stopped, as they almost always did. It was then that Elspeth shared her experience of the previous night with Nikki.

"You were dreaming."

"No, dammit! Come on, Nikki, I'd believe you if you told *me* that!"

"Well, if it's true, what do you think it was?"

"I think it was the dog that lives in that house," she replied, looking past the wrought-iron fence at the old yellow house, which seemed almost benign in the midday sun.

"If you're right, that's not good."

"*I'm right*. It *was* that dog."

"What are you going to do? What if it keeps coming back? What if it..."

"I don't know. I don't think my parents believed me. They thought I had a dream, like you think I did. Have you ever had something bad happen to you and nobody believes you about it? Makes me want to just give up. And it makes me want to never tell anybody anything ever again."

"Well, it didn't hurt you."

"No. Not *last* night. But if it comes back..."

The girls eventually found their way to the Clarke house. 234 Bax Street. The site of Damon's death. The place where their friend had last been alive. Elspeth had never seen it up close like this before.

There was a chain link fence in front of it that stretched across many of the nearby homes, which only had open spaces to allow for walkways. The Clarke mailbox, with black decals on the side saying "234," was dented, and the red flag was raised. A couple of toys were scattered around on the narrow front lawn, including an overturned big wheel and some large plastic blocks. Probably for Damon's little brother, Elspeth figured. The house itself was rather plain and square and painted white, badly needing a new coat.

"I feel so bad for his brother," Nikki said.

"I'm scared for him," Elspeth replied.

"Well, we can't do anything about..."

"I *did* do something about it. The card? Telling Daddy? Telling the police? Maybe it won't help, but at least...oh, look – isn't that him?"

A tow-headed boy of four or five, wearing a dirty striped shirt, had just popped through the front door and began kicking a large plastic ball around the yard. When it bounced off a maple tree, he held his clenched fists in the air and shouted, "Goal!" But his mouth promptly clamped shut when he caught sight of the two girls watching him.

"Hi," Nikki said, approaching the fence. The boy backed away, not speaking. "Are you Damon's little brother?"

He did not answer. Rather, he glowered at her. Elspeth said to Nikki, "We better leave him alone. His father will probably get mad if we talk to him."

Their conversation was interrupted by another boy, who had pushed his way up to them while riding a skateboard. "Hi, Elspeth. Nikki."

"Hi, Patrick!" Elspeth said.

"How come you two are here?"

"Nothing much, we just wanted to look at Damon's house. *I* wanted to look at it."

"Nothing to see," Patrick said. "Just looking at it, you'd never guess what happened in there. Sorta like people...like Mr. Clarke. You can't tell by looking."

"That's his little brother, right?"

"Freddie. Yeah. Hi, Freddie!" Patrick called.

The boy slowly approached the fence. "Hi, Patrick."

"Whatcha doin'?"

"Just playin'."

"Wanna kick the ball back and forth with me?"

"Nah, that's okay," the little boy said.

"Aw, come on, share the ball with me." Freddie looked at him with suspicion, so Patrick asked, "You know what sharing is, right?"

"Sure. It's when everybody has the same much."

The girls giggled while Patrick went on: "Yeah, that's right. Just share the ball with me for a few minutes, okay?" He turned to the girls. "Want to join us?"

Elspeth said, "I can't run well with this leg..."

"Oh yeah, sorry..." Patrick and Freddie kicked the ball to each other for a short time while the girls looked on. Then he said, "See ya, Freddie!" and Freddie waved. Once back on the sidewalk, Patrick asked, "Wanna go to the mall with me?"

The girls looked at each other, and Nikki said, "Well, that's a pretty far walk. We'd get in a lot of trouble if..."

Elspeth cut her off. "Patrick, did the police come to

your house?"

"Yeah! Yours, too?"

"Uh-huh. He asked me a lot of questions."

"Me, too. No big deal. So, come on...let's go to the mall...it's not *that* far."

"How come the police didn't visit *me*?" Nikki interjected. "I went into the old house, too."

"It wasn't about the house, though," Patrick explained. "It was about Damon and his mother getting beaten up. Anyway, you guys coming or not?"

"What do you think, Nik? Let's go there!"

Nikki was outvoted and reluctantly went along.

Chapter 20
Bonding With Patrick...and Again With Nikki

The walk to the mall meant that they'd have to go to the corner again, but instead of turning left as if heading home, they crossed the street and continued along Beechum in the opposite direction. The shopping mall was about a half mile from there. Along the way, Patrick occasionally hopped upon his skateboard and zoomed out ahead of the girls before stopping to kick it upright and carry it under his arm again.

"Showing off," Nikki said, as they caught up to him.

"He's really good on that, though," Elspeth said.

Nearing the mall, Elspeth decided to fill Patrick in on what had happened in her bedroom the previous night. "That's really pretty scary," he said with an uncharacteristically quiet voice, but without a hint of sarcasm.

Sensing his support, Elspeth continued. "Yeah, and nobody believes me."

"I do."

In that instant, Patrick looked to Elspeth like an entirely different person. Like a long-lost, second-best friend. Like someone she could trust. "Thanks."

"There's a CD that I want to buy while we're here, but if there's something you two want to do..."

"I didn't bring any money," Elspeth said.

"I didn't, either," Nikki added. "We'll just, like, go where you go."

"Here," he said, handing them each a dollar bill. "You guys play a game in the arcade while I'm in the store. Just stay there and I'll meet you when I'm done."

"Jeez, thanks, Patrick!" Nikki said.

Elspeth gave him a quick kiss on his cheek, and the girls broke away toward the arcade.

On the way back from the mall with Patrick, having scored poorly on the game they played, Elspeth said, "That was really nice of you to spend your money on us. I mean, we both have money at home..."

"Don't sweat it. I get five dollars from a neighbor for mowing her lawn every week in the summer. I usually buy music with it," he explained, holding up a brown bag. "So, Elspeth...about the dog. You're afraid it'll come back to your house, aren't you?"

"Yeah, I am."

"But it didn't hurt you."

"No...But it scared me a lot. I don't know if I'll ever go to sleep again. Mom and Dad think I'm imagining it."

"Well, parents don't believe us very much. My mom thought I was crazy at first when I told her about Damon being carried away on a stretcher. You know what you should do? You need to prove to them that there really is a dog. Seriously, what you ought to do is go to the house again, but this time with a camera. I'll go with you. How about you, Nikki?"

Nikki loudly piped in, "Oh-h, no-o. Not again!"

"Well, how about it, Elspeth? We can sneak in during the daytime when nobody's looking."

"But it's invisible, Patrick. A camera wouldn't work."

Nikki lost her cool. "That's it! Let's go!" she cried, pulling Elspeth along by the sleeve. "And let's start walking home from school on the *other* side of the street from the house..."

"I've told you to stop pulling me, Nik."

"What are you doing tomorrow, Elspeth?" Patrick asked. Nikki glowered.

"Nothing after church, except lunch. I'll be home."

"Why don't you meet me at the gate of the old house. Say, two o'clock?" Without waiting for her answer, Patrick called back, "At two, then," as he skated toward his house.

"I still say you're crazy," Nikki said, as the girls continued on toward home. Elspeth looked back over her shoulder.

And Patrick looked over his.

"I really like him," Elspeth said.

"He's okay, I guess."

"Are you mad at me, Nik?"

"About what? No!"

Continuing toward home, Elspeth said, "You know you're still my best friend...*ever*."

"I just think he's full of himself, with that dumb skateboard and everything."

"Nik, I really think boys are like that a lot. You just don't know too many of them, that's all. 'Course, I don't either. But I hope you aren't gonna get jealous or something..."

Nikki stopped walking and faced Elspeth. "I'm not

jealous, 'Speth. I just don't..." Elspeth noticed that Nikki's lips were starting to quiver. "I don't want you getting into trouble because he talked you into going back to that house. Besides, you said you were scared by the dog that came into your room. Why would you want to go looking for it in that house again?"

"Like Patrick said, it didn't *hurt* me."

"Bull! It was licking your face last night to see if you tasted good. It's probably pretty hungry, right?"

Elspeth shuddered. Maybe she shouldn't go back inside the house. Maybe she'd just meet Patrick at the gate and let him go in by himself, if he really wanted to. She embraced her friend, and Nikki squeezed her tightly. "Come with me tomorrow...I might change my mind and not go in there." Elspeth could feel Nikki's body contracting and knew that she was crying. "Listen, I promise I won't go back into the house if it worries you."

"It *does* worry me."

"So, just walk to the corner with me, and I'll tell Patrick I'm not going to do it," she assured Nikki, secretly relieved by her decision. "I *want* you to be with me when I tell him. I would miss you if you weren't there."

"You would?"

"I swear."

"Okay," Nikki said, slowly pulling back so that she could wipe her eyes.

"And don't ever worry about Patrick...or anybody else...you're *always* my best friend."

"Thanks, 'Speth," she said, as they walked on to their homes.

Chapter 21
No More Visitors Wanted

"Can I sleep in your bed again tonight?" Elspeth asked her parents during dinner.

Dad looked at Mom and said, "I don't think that's a good idea. But you can leave your door open and the bathroom light on, and we'll leave our door open..."

"But, Daddy, that just makes it easier for the dog to see its way around and..."

"Little Squirrel, listen, okay?" Dad interrupted, more or less patiently. "Dreams can sometimes seem very real, like they're actually happening. I can still remember when I was your age..."

"Dad!" Elspeth demanded. "I'm not a little infant and I'm *not* making this up! And I don't want you to call me Little Squirrel anymore. I'm almost eleven!"

Mom weighed-in. "Honey, why don't we let her stay with us just one more night?"

Dad was growing agitated. "Sure, one night...then two, then three..."

"No, Daddy, I *promise*. Just tonight."

"No."

"All right, Ray, I'll stay with Elspeth in *her* room." Elspeth smiled gratefully at her mom.

"Sally, I just..." Dad stared at his uneaten food and placed his hands flat on the table, taking several deep breaths. "All right...yet again I'm outnumbered by the women of the house." Looking up at his daughter, he said, "Just *one more night* with us, then you have to stay in your own room. Deal? You can't renege on this."

"Yeah, deal! Thank you, Daddy. And you can call me Little Squirrel if you want. I sorta still like it, just not in front of my friends. At least, I like it better than Peg-leg."

Dad saw a way to diffuse the tension. "You know what kids used to call *me* in school?"

Elspeth's face was drawn-in with anticipation. "What?"

"Amy."

"*Amy?*"

"From 'Amesbury.' They kidded me relentlessly with that. But, bullies will find a way to turn any name into an insult, or find something different to pick on you about. No one is safe. You just have to try to let it roll off, even though you're boiling with anger."

"Were you ever boiling with anger?"

"Oh, Lord, yes! I probably cracked a few teeth trying to keep from exploding a few times."

"I didn't think *you* ever got bullied."

"I'll bet there isn't a person on this planet who hasn't been."

"Thanks again, Daddy. After dinner, I guess I'll get ready for bed and read for a while."

Elspeth was sure that falling asleep would be a cinch tonight. Her parents' bedroom door would be closed. Nothing could get inside. She was still overtired from the previous night, and quickly closed her eyes, snuggling tightly beneath the sheets on her mom's side of the bed, lying flat on her stomach. Her face hung a bit over the edge, and her left arm dangled from it.

Mom and Dad were confident Elspeth was asleep when they came into the room a couple of hours later. They carried on a whispered conversation after turning off the bedside light. "That was a good save tonight, Ray. She just needed that support."

"But, you know, I think she's bipolar now, or something," Dad said.

"Like I said, it's just a phase. She's been thinking about the accident again lately, plus she heard us fighting about her the other night."

"I know...I get that...but she's just hanging on to this fantasy of hers. She might not be *able* to stay alone in her own room now. *Then* what? We can't have her sleeping with us anymore. I almost fell off the bed last night because she kept flopping around and pushing me to the side. I really think she should see someone, Sally."

"I agree with you about the first part. I think she needs to be in her own room. But I really don't think she's...I don't think she needs outside help. She's been under a lot of stress lately."

"Oh, and *we* haven't?"

"Yes, but we're the grown-ups, and she's the child. Be a bit more generous toward her. Think back to when you were little and had nightmares and wet your bed and worried about your parents arguing. Just give her love and time, and I think she'll get through this. Hopefully we can *all* get through it. Okay?"

Dad rolled over onto his left side, and said, "I'll try. I really will. But if she doesn't pull out of this attitude or condition or whatever it is soon, you need to agree to have someone on the outside intervene. We aren't equipped for this."

"We're equipped for it, Ray. She's our daughter. We've brought her up for over ten years, and we're going to keep bringing her up. I know your heart was set on having a boy ten years ago, but don't take it out on her. After all, it was your decision not to have any more children after the accident."

"Don't start on that again – it has nothing to do with this. Please. I'm tired." Dad simply shut his mouth at this point and filled his head with thoughts of two big accounts he was working on. Soon he was snoring.

Elspeth had been listening to her parents talking all this time, and now she knew that Daddy had wanted a boy, but he got her instead. And now, a cripple, too. How she was able to sleep at all is anyone's guess, but she did finally drift off.

A while later, her eyes flashed open.

Her dad was out cold. She felt heat from her mom beside her, and the movement of her breathing. She glanced toward the bedroom door and saw, barely, that it was closed, and she settled in to go back to sleep.

But there was something in the room. Not Lucie.

She heard no padding of feet, no panting, no sniffing. The table clock read 2:28. The digits emitted only a faint red light, but she was certain she could see a form, blacker than black, soundlessly circling the bed, back and forth. She could make out no eyes, no ears, no mouth...just a long, lithe outline. This was the same sort of visage she thought she'd seen for a few seconds at the old lady's house on Halloween. It's looking for *me*. Again.

She wanted her parents to be awake to share this occurrence...*then* they'd believe her! She softly poked her mother, who did not immediately respond. She didn't dare speak for fear of startling the creature, which was still silently pacing. She nudged her mother with her elbow, and finally roused her. "What...is that you, Elspeth...?"

"Shh." Elspeth twisted around slowly and talked close to her mother's ear. "Mom, it's in *here*. The dog. It's in the room. Right now!"

Mom did not answer out loud. Instead, she turned her head from the pillow so that she could listen with both ears.

"You probably can't *hear* it, Mom...but watch where the clock light is shining."

Mom shivered. She thought she saw something moving very close to Elspeth, something that she could not define. A shape, but an indistinct one. She felt the hair rising on her arms. For the longest time, mother and daughter lay motionless. Then Mom turned on the light above the bed. Absolutely nothing was in view that didn't belong there: just the two bookshelves, two bureaus, a dresser, a full-length mirror, and a pair of wicker chairs.

But, through the corner of her eye, Elspeth saw a minuscule movement of the door to the walk-in closet. "Mom!" she said out loud. *"It's in the closet."*

Mom thought (but wasn't sure) she had seen the door slide a fraction of an inch. What she knew for certain was that the closet door had been barely open when they all went to bed that night, and now it was open wide enough for...what?

"I'm scared, Mom," Elspeth said, clinging tightly to her mother.

Mom was thinking: what if there's a burglar hiding in there? But, then, why would the door to the hallway still be closed? She pushed her husband's arm, waking him.

"What...what's...?" It took Dad a minute to fully wake up. "What are you doing, Sally?"

"Shh...I think there is...something in our closet."

Dad shook his head to wake himself. "Are you serious?" he whispered.

"Would you please check it?"

"Oh, great, so you girls are king of the house until there's a problem, then Daddy gets to take care of it."

Dad looked at the closet door, which was open about two feet wide. He threw his legs over the side of the bed and stood up. "Well, I can't very well get the gun...it's *in* the closet."

For several moments, all three remained still and listened. Then he slowly crossed the bedroom to the closet, while Mom and Elspeth held their breaths.

"Who's there? I have a gun!"

Elspeth buried her face against her mother, not wanting to look. Mom held her especially tight. "Ray, be careful..."

"Oh, thanks for the tip, honey." Noiselessly, Dad slid the closet door open all the way, which turned the inside light on, and could see nothing out of the ordinary. His dress shirts and suits hanging on one side, Mom's dresses and pant suits on the other. There were a few tall, plastic storage bags hanging up that contained still more clothing...Elspeth had sneaked in there and unzipped one once and was repelled by the smell of moth balls.

But there was nothing alive in the closet. Except for Dad.

"All right, ladies, you got me up," he said, glancing at the clock, "at nearly three in the morning. What on earth *for*? And why am I still whispering?"

"Daddy, that dog was in here. It must have walked right through the bedroom door. Or it could have been hiding in your closet until we went to bed."

"Then, where is it now? Do you see anything here? *A-n-y*thing? And you two aren't being logical. If it just walked through the outside wall into our house, and then right through the bedroom door without opening it, why would it need to open the closet door to get in *there*?"

Mom and Elspeth said nothing, and looked guilty, of what they did not know.

"I have to be in the office by eight o'clock. I'd appreciate it if you would allow me a couple more hours of sleep." He crawled back under his covers and turned on his side, away from his wife and daughter.

Mom helped Elspeth lie back down after fluffing her pillow. "It's okay, sweetie. Let's get some rest now, okay?"

In truth, Mom wasn't completely sure that something hadn't been in the room with them.

Chapter 22
It's All in the Wrist

Sunday afternoon, Elspeth and Nikki set off along the sidewalk of Beechum Street on their way to meet Patrick at the old house. Then, Elspeth stopped, sat against a tree in front of a neighbor's yard, and turned down the sleeve covering her knee and upper portion of the prosthesis. Nikki had walked far ahead of her before realizing she was talking to no one. Her friend was bent-over and doing something to her leg. "C'mon, 'Speth...move your buns!"

"Move them where? To my knees?" Nikki walked back toward Elspeth. "I've got an itch that won't go away. I have to scratch it. No big deal."

Elspeth rolled down several layers of white socks and the liner before popping off the leg so she could reach the bare skin of her stump. Her eyes closed, a smile formed, and she took a deep breath, exhaling with a sigh. "That feels...so...good... You know what's weird? Sometimes I'm sure I feel an itch or a pain way down here," she said, pointing to where her real lower leg used to be. "Impossible, right? The doctor said it's normal." The moment she stopped scratching, she said, "Oh, great...now I've made it sore! I don't think I want to go to the house. Not today."

"Yeah, I agree."

"Dad's gonna get me a new prosthesis again this year because I'm still growing. I get one about every year. I think this is the fourth one I've had...he said it cost nine thousand dollars!"

"Yeah, my braces cost about five thousand, I think. And next year, I'm gonna have to wear a retainer. I wish my teeth would all just fall out."

"No, you don't. You'd have dentures and have to keep them in a glass every night, like Grandpapa did before he died. Really gross."

"Hey...I just had an idea," Nikki said. "You know that we have a holiday weekend next week, right?"

"No...what holiday?"

"It's Veteran's Day. My dad is a vet, so I always know when Veteran's Day is. Well, it's on Saturday, but we celebrate it on Friday, so, no school! Long weekend!"

"Oh, cool."

"And all this week is supposed to be like summer. So, anyway, I have an idea...remember I told you that Dad bought me a little tent last summer for going camping? Well, I mean, we can set it up in my backyard and have an outdoor sleepover!"

"That would be awesome!" Elspeth said, revealing her dimple with a smile. "I could bring my sleeping bag."

"Right! I'll get my parents to say yes. Right now! Let's go to my back yard and we can pick out a place to put the tent. Patrick will find us."

"Good idea," Elspeth said, while fitting her stump back into the plastic leg. "Give me a hand." Nikki pulled Elspeth up to her feet, and the girls walked two blocks back the way they had come, turning into Nikki's driveway. Mrs. Pettengill was watering some late-blooming dahlias with a garden hose. "Hi, girls," she said. "I thought you were going to meet up with your friend from school."

"We decided not to," Nikki told her. "He knows where we live. He'll find us. Hey, Mom, if it's this warm on Friday, can 'Speth and I set up my tent in the yard and sleep outside?"

"It could get quite cold at night, even if the day is warm. This is November, remember."

"Yeah, Mom, like, we *know* that. So can we?"

"Dad's around back doing some trimming...go ask him. If he's okay with it, then it's all right with me."

Nikki lived in a single-story ranch house with light green siding and a small porch at the top of four red brick steps. The lawn was well-kept and outlined by gardens of lilac bushes and forsythia planted beneath layers of cedar chips. These were no longer in bloom, but they'd been carefully trimmed and gave the entire outside of the house an inviting cottage-like quality. "C'mon, 'Speth..."

In the back yard, at the bottom of a shallow hill, Mr. Pettengill was relaxing in a plastic Adirondack chair, wiping sweat from his forehead and sipping a cool drink. "Well, hello, Miss Amesbury. How are you?"

"I'm good, sir. Thank you."

"And your parents?"

"They're both good. Thank you."

"You girls want some lemonade?"

"No thanks."

"I will!" Elspeth said, and was handed a paper cup

full.

"Dad, remember the tent you bought me so we could go camping?"

"Sure. It's in the basement. Sorry we never had the chance to..."

"Elspeth and I want to use it on Friday...we want to set it up here in the back yard."

"Friday? Oh, Friday's a holiday...right. Well, as long as the weather's still nice, I don't have a problem with it. But better clear it with your mother first. And, do you know how to set up a tent?" Both girls shook their heads. "I'll put it together and leave it on the grass back here."

"Great, Dad! Thanks!"

"Are you girls here to help me trim the bushes?"

Nikki said, "No...we just wanted to ask you about the tent."

Nikki took Elspeth's arm and they started around the house toward the front lawn. Elspeth called over her shoulder, "Thank you, Mr. Pettengill!" Then to Nikki she said, "Don't take this wrong, but it's *really* irritating when you keep grabbing my arm and leading me places. I have two legs. Well, one-and-a-half."

"Sorry," Nikki said, letting go of Elspeth's arm but feeling a little hurt.

As they crossed the front lawn, Patrick appeared in the driveway on his bike. "Hey, ah...you were going to meet me at noon by the..."

"Yeah, well, Elspeth's leg was sore."

"We were on our way to meet you, but I had to take off my leg for a few minutes."

"Well, you wanna go now? To the house?"

Elspeth said, "You know what? No."

"Okay...can I ask *why* not?"

"If that thing in the old house is the same as the one that's been visiting me at night – *twice* – I don't want to meet it again. We should just leave it alone. Maybe it'll stop scaring me."

"Well, okay. I really don't care, anyway. I'll go in there by myself. So, unless you have something else in mind, I guess I'll leave now."

"Hey," Nikki said, as a gesture of her acceptance of Patrick, for Elspeth's sake, "you wanna come over on Friday and hang around for an hour or so in our back lawn?"

"What for? You having a party or something?"

"Nope...Dad's gonna set up a tent and 'Speth and I are going to sleep outside. You could come over for a while and we could tell stories and things."

"Hmm. Maybe. I'd have to make something up to tell Mom. But she usually doesn't care where I go."

"It gets dark at about five since we set the clocks back, and we eat at six, so you could just tap on the tent flap at about seven, and we'll come out and sit on the grass and talk. Bring a flashlight. We have to keep it quiet. And you can only stay until we get tired."

"That sounds cool. We can talk about it more at lunch tomorrow. Hey...wanna see something?" Patrick shoved a still-golden-tan arm into his pants pocket and produced a quarter. "Now, this is just a regular quarter. You can check it if you want."

"That's all right," Elspeth said. "We believe you."

"And I'm wearing short sleeves, so you know I won't be hiding it in my shirt." Patrick clenched his fist around the quarter. "Nikki...blow on my hand."

Nikki took an enormous breath, as though preparing to blow out birthday candles, and let it burst against his fingers, which he unfolded one at a time, revealing an empty palm.

Elspeth was awe-struck. "How did you *do* that?"

"It's all in the wrist," he said.

"What do ya mean?" Nikki asked.

"Things are never what they seem to be with magic. They call it 'misunderstanding...' no, no. 'Mis*direction*.' While I'm doing the *real* trick, you're still watching for the quarter. Sleight of hand. Not the truth." Patrick reached to Nikki's left ear, and seemingly pulled the missing quarter from it. "I've got a whole bunch of tricks I'm learning. That's the first one. Pretty good, huh? But you can't keep the quarter."

"Show us some more when you learn them!"

"Okay. But I won't ever tell you how I do them, so don't ask. Anyway, see you guys," Patrick said, turning his back to the girls and peddling on toward his home on Bax Street.

Damon's obituary on page 23 of the Sunday paper was four days late being published. But, on the front page that very same morning, was the much more timely announcement of Mr. Clarke's indictment for 'alleged domestic abuse.' Elspeth's mom was reading it after breakfast as her husband devoured his toast and jelly. "Honey...look at this."

She shook her head, lamenting the death of this young boy, yet *still* the paper did not reveal what had actually caused it. Apparently, Mr. Clarke had beaten his wife the same night that Damon died, but

Damon's name wasn't mentioned in the front page story at all.

A memorial service for Damon was announced for Thursday at the church on Bax Street, and Mom decided she would offer to take Elspeth. It was after school, anyway. "You don't have to go," Mom said, putting a plate of toast and jelly in front of her.

"I'll go. I *want* to. Nikki probably will, too. She could go with us. And I'm sleeping over in her new tent Friday night."

Mom glanced at her with narrowed eyes. "You'll be doing this with *whose* permission?"

"Yours! Yours and Daddy's. Is it okay? *Please*... We'll stay right in Nikki's backyard."

"I'll give her mom a call. If she says it's okay, then it's okay."

In other words, as usual, Elspeth got what she wanted.

Chapter 23
In Memoriam

Whatever had been visiting Elspeth's home did not return on Sunday night, nor on Monday or Tuesday night. Elspeth was beginning to second-guess herself. Had anything *really* come into her room, or into her parents' room? Sure, she had a broad imagination, but those visits seemed...so...real.

In any case, Elspeth was grateful that she was able to get some sleep now, and that the tension between her and her parents had died down to almost nothing. She had her Friday sleepover at Nikki's to look forward to, and was even sort of looking forward to Damon's memorial service tomorrow, if only to add her support for his mother and little brother.

During school lunch, Elspeth and Nikki rather blithely carried their trays right up to the boys' table in the back, just to see whether or not they'd still be welcome there. A couple of the boys slid over right away to let the girls in. "I don't know what this is," Elspeth said, putting her tray down, "but I'm hungry, so I guess I'll eat it."

"Some kind of casserole," Patrick said.

"Well, it *looks* like something that got stuck in our garbage disposal," Elspeth said. "And it smells like Lucie's litter box."

"You guys should have gone to the house with me Sunday," Patrick said. "I heard that dog you talked about."

"You went in by yourself?" one of Patrick's friends asked.

"Yeah...wasn't so bad. But I think there really is a dog in there. Anyway, *some*thing growled at me, so I left. But I'll go back, if anybody will come with me."

The other boys at the table seemed to be in awe of Patrick, and their eyes popped at the idea that he'd confronted something like that by himself...and in *that* house. But then, Patrick became subdued. "Damon wanted to get another dog after his got killed, but his dad told him no more pets. Poor Freddie...no one to play with now, except me. That's why I go next door most days after school and kick the ball around with him. As long as Mr. Clarke isn't home. He's still in jail. But I'm sure he'll get out."

"Not if he beat up Mrs. Clarke...I mean, they wouldn't let him come back home now, would they?" Nikki asked.

Elspeth took a poll. "Who's going to Damon's funeral service tomorrow?" A couple of the boys said they were, but Patrick did not answer. "You going?" Elspeth asked, singling him out.

"I dunno. Maybe."

Nikki, sounding rather self-righteous, said, "You guys were best friends. You *gotta* go!"

"I don't *gotta*," Patrick told her, firmly. "Don't tell me I *gotta*, Nikki." Embarrassed, Nikki backed off quickly, casting her eyes down toward a tray full of lunch she had no appetite for. Patrick spit a half-mouthful of food back onto his plate. "That is so disgusting. I keep forgetting to make a bag lunch."

"Wouldn't your mom do that?" Elspeth asked.

"She's never up that early."

"Your dad, maybe?"

"He died when I was two...I thought I told you that already. Well, everyone else here knows it." Anxious to change the subject, he said, "I might go to the funeral, I dunno."

Elspeth said, "It's only for an hour or so, right?"

"Yeah, well...like I said, I *might* go."

Patrick did attend Damon's memorial service, but sat in the back. There were a few kids present whom Nikki and Elspeth knew from their classes, but there were mostly grown-ups. Mrs. Clarke was greeting people who walked through the door of the church, trying to put on an optimistic face, and receiving a lot of hugs. This was not the church that Elspeth went to each week, and she was not familiar with the pastor, who stood behind a long table covered by a light-blue cloth that was decorated with flower arrangements. Displayed on the table were more than two dozen upright frames holding photos. Damon was in all of them. His mom and Freddie were in many of them. Damon's big golden retriever was in a few.

Mr. Clarke was in none of them. Not one.

"Friends, this is a time to both grieve and rejoice. We grieve that one of our younger and more vulnerable citizens has left our sides, although not in spirit. And we rejoice because he was a part of our community and our friend for ten years."

For the most part, the few kids attending the service from fourth grade had dressed in the clothes they wore to school, including Patrick, who wore a long-sleeve t-shirt, denim jeans, and sneakers. Elspeth was speculating that they were mostly Bax Street neighbors of Damon's and not from Beechum, her street. Kids from her neighborhood would certainly be dressed nicer, like she was in her pressed slacks and turtleneck sweater, and Nikki in her plaid dress and pullover shirt. But, as she glanced over to Mrs. Clarke, who was certainly dressed the best she was able with what little she had, Elspeth shamed herself for comparing herself to the others.

She had half-wanted to see Damon one last time, even if he was dead in a casket, but there was no casket on view. Then she decided it was better that she *not* see him. He'd be pale white, eyes shut forever, lying in a box with wonderful, frilly lining that would benefit him not in the least. Why do they bother with all that? she wondered. It wasn't as though the dead person inside would feel more comfortable. Probably costs a fortune.

She and Nikki sat together in a pew between Elspeth's parents. Ahead of her in the front row, Elspeth watched little Freddie, kicking his feet restlessly while his mother kept trying to calm him. The girls paid almost no attention to what the pastor said, being quite absorbed with the whole surreal mood of the service.

Elspeth made it a point to go to Damon's mother after the service and place her hand upon the distraught woman's arm. "We all miss Damon, Mrs. Clarke. He was really one of our best friends."

Freddie was not old enough to understand how discourteous it was of him to just enter into the conversation. "He's gonna get put under the ground!" he announced, apparently proud that he knew this all by himself. "Yup, and he's going to be there for*ever* from now on."

Elspeth shivered. Yeah...forever.

Mrs. Clarke took her son firmly by the shoulders. "Freddie, that is not polite. You promised you'd be good, remember...?"

"I *am* being good," Freddie insisted. "Better than Daddy!"

Mrs. Clarke took the preschooler by the hand and led him hastily away, but not before thanking Elspeth and Nikki for their support and for the card Elspeth's class had sent to her. "You are wonderful girls. Damon would be so proud of you right now," she said, now audibly weeping into a handkerchief and walking with Freddie through the door and into the beautiful November afternoon.

Chapter 24
Daddy Time

Following the funeral service, Elspeth was thinking about Freddie, about how he should have a dog, or at least be able to play with one sometimes. It occurred to her then that *she* really wanted a dog, too, so her campaign began. "Daddy, can we go to the shelter and look for a puppy?"

Dad was sitting in his favorite chair in the living room after dinner, his legs sprawled and arms outstretched as he yawned. "Honey, that was great pot roast. Of course, now I can't move."

"Yeah," Elspeth agreed. "It was really good. Especially the gravy for the mashed potatoes. Mom, you should work in the school kitchen."

"Well, thank you, sweetie, but even if I did, you'd still be getting fish sticks and meat loaf. For dinner at home, I try to do better."

"So, Daddy, can we get a dog?" Elspeth, already in her pajamas, was playfully leaning into, then pushing away from, the arm of Dad's chair. "Can we get *two* puppies?"

Dad frowned a bit. "*Two?* Why two?"

"I want us to get one for Freddie."

"Who?"

"Damon's little brother Freddie. He misses his dog because his dad killed it. He should have someone to play with."

"First, Little Squirrel, we don't even know if the shelter would have *one* puppy, let alone two. And we don't know if any puppy you bring home would get along with Lucie. And we don't know that Mr. Clarke wouldn't..."

"Yeah, hurt the puppy, too. But, Daddy, he's in jail now."

"We don't know how long he'll be there. And, have you talked this over with Freddie's mother? Maybe she doesn't want..."

"She already told Patrick that Freddie really misses their dog. She sounded like she really wanted him to have another one."

"Then, I think it would be proper to let her make the decision, and to go pick out a new dog with Freddie instead of you choosing for him. Don't you?"

Elspeth hung her head a little. "I 'spose."

"And they may not be ready for a puppy right now. They've had a lot of tragedy and turmoil in their home. They probably need time. And *we* may not be ready for a puppy right now, either. You have never had to take care of an animal that needs to be exercised every day and fed twice a day and..."

"I can! I promise I will!"

"You would have to pick up its poop wherever you walk it, and always carry little bags..."

"Yes, I will!"

"You have to groom it...brush its coat and give it baths..."

"I will!"

"It would probably shed a lot, so you would need to do a lot of vacuuming."

"I like to vacuum anyway."

"And what about the dog in that old house? Are you finally going to let go of your idea that it's a ghost that haunts your bedroom?"

"And *your* bedroom?" Elspeth said, sensing she could easily lose this argument. "But it hasn't come back for a while."

"So, if we go to the shelter, would you promise not to mention that other dog again?"

Elspeth felt trapped. What if the dog *did* come back some night? Would she have to break a promise and mention it? "I... can't promise, Daddy. I'll *try* not to."

"C'mere, kid," Dad said, holding out his arms and pulling Elspeth to him in a long, loving hug. "You are just what your mom said you are...a kind and generous little person who thinks of other people and animals more than about yourself. Don't ever lose that, and you will always make friends easily."

"But, I *don't* make friends easily, Daddy. I hardly make them *at all*."

"Well, do you think you would have been able to get all of your classmates to sign that card if they didn't like you?"

"Um..."

"And who was Damon, if not your friend? And what about Patrick and Nikki? If you're thinking about your leg, I understand that. Part of you is missing and some people will find that a turn-off and some people will giggle behind your back and make jokes. But those are just *little* people...over time *they're* the ones who won't make friends easily. Does that make sense?"

"I guess...but Dad, how can a father be so mean to

people and animals? So mean that he kills them? They're his *family*!"

"Let's go for a walk. Just you and me."

"It's already dark, Daddy."

"So what? Come on, Little Squirrel – put on a sweater or a jacket and we'll walk to the end of the street. Okay?"

"But I'm wearing pajamas!"

"Well, how many people do you think we'll meet on the sidewalk at this hour? Besides, it's still pretty warm out."

Elspeth grabbed a jacket from the closet, not wanting to pass up some private Daddy time.

"Have a good walk, you two," Mom said as they went through the front door.

Father and daughter walked past two streetlights without talking as they took in the idyllic stillness, and cool redolence of the air. "You know, some grown-ups do things they're very ashamed of later," Elspeth's father said. "I'm sure that, whatever Mr. Clarke did, he'll have to live with it in his memory forever."

"But, how could he *do* it? To people he's supposed to *love*?"

"You know, Elspeth, sometimes we hurt the people we love the most. And the people who we think are heroes...we sometimes believe they only have a good side. But good people can do awful things...even to their own families...even to their kids."

"But does drinking make *everyone* get mean like he does?"

"Some people don't handle drinking well, and they should not be doing it. It seems Mr. Clarke should not have been drinking. But there's no law to stop him from doing it."

"Daddy?"

"Hmm?"

"Do you ever drink?"

"Not alcohol...not anymore."

"You mean, you used to?"

"Years ago. I stopped."

"Did you ever get mean while you were drinking?"

"I don't think so. Your mother never said that I did, but..."

That "but" hung in the evening air like a bubble begging to be popped.

"What, Daddy?"

"Elspeth, I've been thinking a lot about you the past few weeks while all of this commotion has been going on...your friend's death, your fear that Mom and I will divorce...this dog you say you've heard. You've made me think about...well, for one thing, how deeply I love you and how much I want to see you succeed at everything you do. I know there will be times when you won't succeed, and that will always break your mother's heart, and mine. But you'll be stronger from that, and your mom and I will be right here together to help you. You're going to make us proud. You already have."

Elspeth took her father's hand and squeezed it with gratitude and relief as they continued along toward the intersection of Bax and Beechum Streets. "I love you too, Daddy."

"But I think it's time to tell you what really happened four years ago."

She thought: four years ago? Oh, yeah...*that*. "But,

I already *know*...that lady ran right through a stop sign and hit our car..."

"No. That lady didn't pass through a stop sign. *I* did."

Elspeth let go of her father's hand, and stopped walking to look up at him. "Huh...?"

"I'd been drinking. I wasn't drunk, really, but I wasn't as fast to react as I should have been...I did not see that other car coming, and because of that, your mom suffered a broken arm and you lost a leg. And you know that dimple on your right cheek when you smile? That also came from the accident. I wasn't even hurt. It was never your fault. It was always just mine."

"Daddy, why didn't you tell me that before?"

"My fault, too. I couldn't do it. I just couldn't explain to a six-year-old that...well, it just got harder to try to tell you every year because you got used to your leg and it didn't seem...I didn't think you would blame yourself."

"Is the accident why you stopped drinking?"

"That's right, sweetheart. On that very day."

She took her father's hand again, but not quite as tightly. "Thanks, Daddy."

"For what, Elspeth?"

"For not drinking anymore. And...I forgive you."

When Dad and Elspeth reached the corner of Bax and Beechum, they stopped and looked past the iron gate toward the old house, which was visible only as an indistinct outline due to the absence of moonlight and the burned-out bulb of the nearest street lamp.

"So, this is where you heard the dog."

"Twice. Once from standing where we are now,

and the other time when we were inside the house on Halloween. Patrick went in by himself on Sunday, and he heard it, too."

Dad focused his eyes toward the house and concentrated with all his will, listening for something other than the rattling of the bare tree branches and passing cars. He was actually hoping he would hear a dog in there. "You weren't imagining it, right?"

"I *swear*. Did that officer guy ever go in there and look around?"

"Detective Todd? I haven't heard. Tell you what, though...we'll go to the shelter soon and see if we can't find a puppy friend for you. Maybe it could scare the bad dog away. Don't know how Lucie's gonna like it. And...you have to promise you'll take care of it. For now, let's go home."

"I'm so sleepy...can you carry me?"

Dad took his daughter into his arms while she wrapped hers around his neck and her legs around his waist. The stubble of his beard against her cheek and the smell of his after shave was reassuring as the two headed back beneath the nine street lights between the intersection and their driveway. She was asleep as they entered through the front door, and Dad brought her upstairs, removed her leg, and tucked her under the bedcovers. "'Night, little one," he said, kissing her forehead, and leaving her door open a crack as always.

Downstairs, he embraced his wife and held her for a long, long time.

Chapter 25
The Camp Out, Part 1 – Patrick's Revelation

It was a bit strange to be camping out long after all the trees had shed their leaves, when there were no fireflies to catch, and no peepers or crickets to help them to sleep. No, this was a night to be spent in a one-person pup tent, occupied by two persons. It would be chilly, and the girls prepared to climb into their sleeping bags very early on, using their flashlights to see each other's face.

Nikki had a big light with a handle on the top, and she showed Elspeth how she could push one button and turn on the really bright front light, and another to turn on a smaller red light. "The red one's so we don't have to wake anyone else up if we have to, like, go out and pee or something. I'll show you. Turn your light off." A moment later, Elspeth heard a click, and the inside of the tent went red. "How cool is that?"

"This reminds me of that house where the old lady was on Halloween night. Remember? All red inside. Spooky." The tent went dark and Elspeth turned her light back on. She removed her right leg, placing it beside her, and snuggled down deep into her bedding.

Nikki said, "That's a really cool sleeping bag. It looks like it's a lot warmer than mine...a lot puffier."

Elspeth shivered and rubbed her arms, even though she wore a heavy sweater and had her sleeping bag pulled up to her neck, because her body heat hadn't kicked in yet. An owl screeched from somewhere in the deep woods on the back edge of Nikki's lawn, behind the tent. A small creature scurried past them before she could train her light on it. Probably a mouse.

But something much heavier than a mouse was also moving across the lawn toward them. "Hey! Nikki...Elspeth...are you in there?" Patrick called, aiming his own flashlight ahead.

Elspeth peeked out. "Yeah, we're in here."

"That's a pretty small tent for the two of you."

"Hey, Patrick...you made it," Nikki said. "I forgot that you might come tonight."

"Listen, I really came here because I have to tell you something. Then I'm going home."

"Well, we're already in our sleeping bags, so you can't come inside."

"I wasn't going to. I'll just throw the flap over the roof and kneel right here and talk to you." Once this was done, Patrick's voice took on a very serious tone. "I think you two are pretty good friends of mine now, and I think I trust you, so I'm going to tell you something. But...*really important*...you can't tell your parents, and you can't share this with friends. I'm not even going to tell the other kids at school. You have to swear, or I won't tell you. Cross your hearts and hope to die." The girls complied. "Okay. Mr. Clarke didn't kill Damon."

"How do you know?"

"I went over to visit Freddie this afternoon. Mrs. Clarke invited me in. She was very sad and she was shaking a little, and her eyes had dark bulges underneath, like she wasn't getting any sleep. She told me something, the same thing I'm telling you now." Patrick shielded his face from Nikki's flashlight. "Turn that off, Nikki. Hurts my eyes."

The tent went dark, then all red with another click of a button. "So, *Mrs*. Clarke killed him?" Elspeth asked.

"No. Freddie did."

There was a very long pause before Nikki said, "You came all the way here tonight just to play a really crumby joke on us? Well, it's not funny. I mean, Freddie's only five years old!"

"He's four, actually. But listen. Mr. Clarke was drunk and left his gun on the kitchen table and started yelling at Damon and Mrs. Clarke. He said he was going to kill them. Freddie just picked up the gun and aimed it at his father like a little kid would...you know, all shaky and not knowing how to hold it right. But his dad stepped out of the way from Damon at just the wrong second, and the bullet hit Damon in the chest. Freddie killed his older brother *while he was trying to save his life!*"

"But *Mr. Clarke* got arrested."

"He got arrested because Mrs. Clarke called 9-1-1 and said Damon was on the kitchen floor bleeding, and she was afraid her husband might hurt Freddie. A rescue truck came with a few police cars, and Damon was already dead. Mr. Clarke was passed out on the couch. They handcuffed him and had to kind of drag him out 'cause he was so drunk. Mrs. Clarke told them everything, and begged them not to let it get in the news about what really happened. And today she told me the whole story, because I was nice to Freddie and 'cause Damon was my best friend. But, you see why you have to keep this a secret?"

After a moment of all three saying nothing, Elspeth expressed what both she and Nikki were thinking: "That's so awful. Freddie must be going crazy about what he did."

"He doesn't really understand what happened. The gun was already cocked when he picked it up, and when it fired it knocked him backwards off his feet. Mrs. Clarke took him out of the kitchen right away, before he could even see his brother lying there. His mom doesn't want him to know what happened until he's older. What Freddie *does* know is that Damon isn't home to play with anymore. Plus no dog. Plus no dad for now, so Mrs. Clarke has to do everything, and she already has a job in town. I offered to babysit Freddie for free, but she thinks I'm too young. She trusted me enough to tell me all that, and asked me to keep it to myself. I just had to tell *some*body, so I'm telling you."

"That poor little kid. And poor Mrs. Clarke," said Elspeth.

"Yeah, well, this isn't supposed to be something anyone knows about, except just us and the police and Mrs. Clarke. Can you imagine what Freddie would have to go through if everybody in Siteson knew he killed his brother? That's probably why the news didn't report it."

"But he was trying to *help* Damon, not hurt him! He couldn't help it if he was only four. Jeez, he could have shot *himself* just as easily. And now what happens to him when Mr. Clarke gets out of jail?"

"I dunno, but I gotta go. Just remember...don't tell

anyone what I just told you! And have an awesome camp out."

Patrick tossed the tent flap back down and the girls inside heard him walking quickly away.

Chapter 26
Camp Out Part 2 - No Mosquitos, Just Something Worse

When Patrick was gone, Elspeth solemnly murmured, "Memento mori."

"Don't say that, 'Speth. It's creepy."

The night sky offered no visible moon, but did display an overhead carpet of velvet black, pocked with stars of several colors and many sizes, some of them twinkling a bit. "The Big Dipper," Nikki pointed out, as the two girls poked their heads through the tent flap and laid on their backs. "That's the only constellation I know. The tip of it aims toward the North Star. And that's Venus, and that..." she said, locating it with her finger, "is Mars. Do you know about any more?"

"Nikki, we can't keep that promise to Patrick..."

"What do you mean? Of *course* we can. We *have* to. We *swore*. You don't really want Freddie to be known around town as the kid who killed his brother, do you?"

"But everyone will think that *Mrs*. Clarke..."

"No! No one has said *how* Damon died. The police must think it's best if Freddie..."

"Shh!"

"What?"

"Patrick's gone home, right?"

"Yeah..."

The girls sat motionless, half-inside their sleeping bags.

"Well, then, there's someone else in the backyard with us," Nikki said. "Or something."

"Zip down the flap, and stay quiet."

The girls huddled in the tent, turning off their lights and listening. Using a very low voice, Elspeth said, "I don't hear anything..."

There was a mild stirring of empty tree twigs tinkling together, but absolutely no other sound. The girls let down their guard just long enough to crawl deeper into their bags.

After a half-hour of rather grim conversation about Freddie, they fell uneasily off to sleep. That is to say, Nikki did. Elspeth lay stubbornly awake, deep in thought about Freddie. "Nik?" she whispered. No sound from her friend except for deep, measured breathing. Pulling one arm out of her sleeping bag, she felt around until she located her prosthesis. Good – it was still there beside her. Of *course* it was, she thought with a quiet giggle...it couldn't just hop out of the tent by itself. Now, *that* would be a sight! But the plastic leg was damp, and the outside of her sleeping bag was damp. Dew was forming on the lawn around them, making her chilly even when she scrunched back inside her bedding, zipping her bag clear to the top, leaving only a small hole for her hand to fit through and for fresh air to get in.

Sounding muffled to her, because her head was inside the bag and the bag was inside the tent, Elspeth could nonetheless hear something carefully stepping on dry leaves just beyond the tree line at the edge of the woods. "Nik? You awake?" She asked again.

Nikki mumbled, "Mmm?"

"Listen." But just then, the crunching of leaves stopped abruptly.

"What is it?" Nikki asked, sleepily.

"I dunno. I guess noth..."

But then the noises started up again, and Nikki sat up like a human springboard. "What *is* that, 'Speth? I'll bet it's just Patrick messing with us."

"Be quiet!"

The footsteps paused every so often, as though who or whatever was making them wanted to find their tent in almost pitch darkness.

"Oh, my god," Nikki said, as panic began to set in.

"If you don't shut up, it's gonna find us!"

For an extended period of time, they made not the tiniest noise. Had Elspeth shown a flashlight on her, she'd have seen Nikki with eyes half the size of her face, which was beginning to sweat in spite of the midnight November chill.

The front of their tent was facing toward the house, and the woods were behind them. There was no flap in the back. The only way to spot any intruder was to crawl out of the tent and shine their lights toward the woods, but they did not dare to do that.

Nikki pushed her bone-dry lips to the hole at the top of Elspeth's sleeping bag and said, "I wanna go inside!"

"I know, Nik, but if we leave the tent..."

The footsteps they'd heard walking on the fallen forest leaves stopped again.

"I'll bet it's on the lawn now...we won't be able to hear it anymore because Dad raked all the...oh,

'Speth, *I'm so scared*!"

There was so much absolute silence that the girls could almost hear their fingernails grow. Nothing could be heard approaching them across the lawn.

Then, something began scratching at the back of the tent, seeking a way inside. "What if it's a bear?" Nikki whispered.

"Do you have your flashlight in your hand?"

"I do *now*," Nikki said, grabbing it from her side.

"Okay, I say we turn on our lights and run to your basement door."

"No, 'Speth...we'll get *attacked*!"

Elspeth realized she was in serious trouble, trying to pull the zipper of her bag down but finding that it would not budge. "Nikki...I can't get out! The zipper's stuck! Help me out!"

Nikki crawled out of her sleeping bag, turned on the red light, and tried to help Elspeth with her zipper, but it was caught on the lining. "I *can't*, 'Speth!"

"Do you have a pocket knife with you?"

"Uh-uh."

The scratching on the tent canvas moved around to the side. Elspeth's side. "Nik, you gotta go to your house and get your parents to help me!"

"*I'm* not going out there!" Nikki replied, as she continued to try to wiggle the zipper loose.

"We have to get out! *Please* help me!"

"Well...how can I...okay, try putting your hands out through the hole so you can at least crawl."

The tapping and scratching from outside continued. "Can you pull me out...just pull me in the sleeping bag up to your house?"

"Are you serious? You're way too heavy, 'Speth!

And that thing out there will eat us alive while I'm trying to pull you!"

The scratching sound rounded the corner from the side of the tent and began clawing at the front, where the flap was.

"What's going on, Nik?"

"It's blocking the flap. I mean...*it's right next to me on the other side!*"

"Can it get in?"

"If it knows how to unzip the flap it can...or if it has really sharp claws..."

Elspeth put her nose and mouth right up to the hole in her bag and screamed, "What *are* you? What do you *want*?" To the surprise of both girls, the scratching at the canvas stopped instantly. "Are you the dog that comes into my house?" Silence from outside. "Do you live in the old house on the corner?" More silence. "Will you let us leave the tent?" For several moments, Nikki and Elspeth stayed perfectly still. "You think it's gone, Nik?"

"I don't hear anything."

"Could you unzip the flap and help me to your house? Just stand me up...I think I can hop in this thing as long as you keep me from falling."

"I don't wanna go out there, 'Speth!"

"C'mon, Nik! We're just sitting ducks in here!"

"You're gonna have to lay flat on your stomach, and I'll pull you out and then get you up on your foot. I mean, like, this is really dangerous..."

"Yeah, it is, and I love for you helping me. Please! We're just cornered in here..."

Nikki very gingerly unzipped the flap and poked her head through. In the red light, she saw something:

a strange outline that was moving silently back and forth in front of her. She quickly turned on the white light, and the shape vanished in an instant. Aiming the beam around the yard, she saw there was nothing but what belonged there. "I think... 'Speth, I *think* I saw something a minute ago, but I must have been hallucinating or something. There's nothing out here."

Elspeth poked her arms through the hole in her bag as far as she could, and Nikki grabbed her hands. Once through the flap, she said, "Okay, help me up. I'll have to come back tomorrow to get my fake leg."

The tension in the air was electric. What if, while they were most vulnerable and halfway up the lawn to Nikki's basement door, the person or creature chose to attack? With her protruding right arm around Nikki's shoulder, Elspeth had to actually hop with alarming clumsiness as she was guided across the yard, resembling a huge upright caterpillar trying to bounce forward on a single hind leg. In other circumstances, the sight of her would have made both girls laugh for hours.

"Keep going, Nik!" Elspeth shouted, sounding like she was talking with a tennis ball in her mouth.

For Nikki, the hardest part of reaching safety was trying to get Elspeth up a short hill with one arm, while holding the flashlight with her other hand. After that it was only a short distance to the Pettengill's cellar door. But the grass was slippery because of the dew that already coated the lawn. Elspeth, awkwardly gaining but a few inches at a time along uneven ground, slipped and fell twice. "Come on! Up!" Nikki said.

Elspeth's bag kept skidding on the dew, and Nikki

finally gave up trying to keep her balanced. Exhausted from their efforts, the girls simply began screaming, shrilly and relentlessly, until lights in Nikki's house, as well as those in a couple of other homes nearby, flicked on, and Mr. Pettengill rounded the corner wearing his robe and slippers. "What on earth is it?"

"Daddy! We have to get inside..."

"Mr. Pettengill...I left my leg in the tent!" Elspeth cried from within her sleeping bag.

"All right, let's get you inside first and I'll go back to get your leg."

Nikki's father ended up carrying Elspeth, nearly slipping and falling himself a couple of times. She was still encased in her bag when at last the three made it safely into Nikki's home.

"What *happened* out there?"

Neither girl had an answer. "I...*we* don't know," Nikki confessed.

"Well, let's get you out of that thing," Nikki's father said, working Elspeth's sleeping bag zipper until at last it came loose from the lining. Elspeth pretty much spilled out of it onto the living room carpet. "Would you like me to call your parents and have them pick you up?"

"No, it's okay. *I'm* okay. Thanks, Mr. Pettengill."

"We can sleep in my room," Nikki said. "I can show Yertle to you, okay?"

Nikki's mother was also up from all the din, and offered the girls a late snack, while her husband went back outside to fetch Elspeth's leg. "Careful, Daddy!" Nikki warned.

Sitting at the kitchen table with milk and brownies

in front of them, Nikki and Elspeth caught their breath and told Mrs. Pettengill what had happened, as much as they were able. "Mom, there was something in the back yard looking for us..."

Then, Mr. Pettengill came through the front door, carrying Nikki's sleeping bag over his shoulder, and a prosthetic leg beneath his arm. "Here you go, honey."

Elspeth thanked Nikki's dad profusely, while mounting the icy-cold leg back onto her stump.

"What did you say was bothering you out there?"

"We dunno," Nikki told him. "Maybe a bear, or maybe a..."

"When I went out to fetch your leg, I saw a lot of...looked like dog tracks in the dew." The girls' faces went white. "They went around the tent and all the way to where I picked Elspeth up from the lawn. They were right *beside* your own tracks. Are you sure you didn't *see* anything?"

Elspeth and Nikki looked at each other, and Elspeth took a deep breath and sighed through pursed lips, her cheeks inflated. She was never going to be rid of this ghost dog curse.

Chapter 27
Learning a Little More

Mom began preparing dinner on Saturday night, with Dad helping, which he often did on weekends. This was to be lasagna night, and Dad was in charge of layering the three kinds of cheese and the meat and the pasta, while mom took care of the sauce. Elspeth was in charge of preparing the salad ingredients, and chopped the romaine lettuce, tomatoes, cucumbers, onions and peppers with a long, very sharp produce knife. She was quite adept at this and had only cut herself once, a long time ago. Recently she had developed an interest in helping prepare and cook the main dish, which her mom said she could try her hand at during her upcoming Thanksgiving vacation.

"Are we still gonna go to the animal shelter for a puppy, Daddy?"

"That's the plan. Your mother and I have talked it over, and we think it would be better to find a dog for you before winter starts. I'll leave a few hours early from work on Monday and pick you up after school while your Mom works at the library." Elspeth's eyes lit up. "But, another thing, Little Squirrel – even if the new dog and Lucie get along at all, you know that Lucie's going to be very jealous. You have to make sure to pay her as much attention as you always do."

"Yes, Daddy, I will."

"But if we bring the puppy home and Lucie won't tolerate it...you know, if she hisses at it and won't go anywhere near it..."

"I know, it will have to go back to the...wait a minute!" Elspeth said, interrupting herself. "We could give it to Freddie, then!"

"Freddie Clarke?"

"Yeah!"

"We talked about this before. They might not be ready..."

"But, we can ask!"

Dinner was put on the table, and Elspeth used the salad tongs to portion her vegetable creation onto the three plates. "Very nice job, sweetie," Mom said, and Elspeth beamed.

They all watched their favorite Saturday night TV show together, Elspeth holding a wooden bowl of freshly-made popcorn, some of which landed on the carpet for Lucie to inhale. "How come David hasn't asked Portia to marry him yet?" she asked, watching the program with wide eyes, and receiving no answer from her parents. "Every week he's *about* to ask her, and then he doesn't. She ought to tell him to either propose to her or go jump in a lake."

The show was followed by the nine o'clock local news. The headline story was about Mr. Clarke. Dad, Mom and Elspeth leaned forward with their full attention. "Abbott Clarke of Bax Street in Siteson is being held without bail for the shooting death of his 10-year-old son, Damon. He was officially charged with the crime this morning after confessing to the investigators that he had been holding the gun when it accidentally fired. Alcohol was allegedly involved."

Elspeth said, "But...*Freddie* did it. It was an accident, but it wasn't Mr. Clarke who shot him...the police *know* that!" Elspeth's parents glared at her with surprise, and she realized she had just broken her promise to Patrick. On the TV, a photo of Mr. Clarke came up on the screen beside the news anchor. He was holding up a sign in front of him that showed his name, the date, and a long prisoner number. He was wearing an orange jump suit, hadn't shaved and looked like he might be a street beggar. His eyes were sad and swollen. Something about that photo stirred pity in Elspeth.

The newscaster continued, "Mr. Clarke had earlier admitted he killed the family's pet dog last summer. If convicted for the boy's death, Mr. Clarke could be facing a sentence of twenty to forty years in prison for second-degree murder." Then, as fast as the story had begun, it ended and a new one came up.

"He didn't *do* it, Daddy. He didn't shoot Damon." Then, as though an electric charge from a lightning bolt had shot through her body, she cried, "*The dog!*"

Elspeth's father, startled, said, "What dog? That dog you keep on saying you...Surely, you don't think the *dog* had anything to do with Damon's...?"

"No! 'Course not! But the dog that kept coming here and then to our tent last night...that dog *was* Damon's! It was Freddie's!" Elspeth was pacing back and forth across the living room floor. "Daddy! It was *Damon's dog*! That's what scratched at our tent last night...that's what was in my bedroom and in your room! It just wanted attention."

Elspeth's parents had heard the story about the

previous night's campout events from the Pettengills, and were told about the canine footprints on the lawn. For a moment, Dad wondered whether his daughter might actually have been haunted by something. But it was a fleeting notion.

"I gotta call Mrs. Clarke!" Elspeth said, moving quickly toward the phone.

"Calm down, Little Squirrel. It's after nine, and Mrs. Clarke is probably watching this news show and feeling really terrible right now..."

"I'll just be a minute."

"No, *put down the phone*." He stood from his chair to interrupt Elspeth's call, but by then Mrs. Clarke's phone was ringing on the other end. Dad stood behind her with his arms folded.

"Mrs. Clarke? This is Elspeth Amesbury. One of Damon's friends. I'm fine, thank you. Um...I was just watching the news... Yes, I know. Yes, ma'am. Do you need anything? Is Freddie okay? I'm really glad to hear that. I just had a question..."

Dad looked at Mom, who turned her hands up in the air, and wore a face that said, "*I* don't know...do *you*?"

"What was his name...the dog's? What did Mr. Clarke do with him after he died?" There was a pause before she said, "Okay, Mrs. Clarke...I'm really sorry to bother you, but it was important for me to know. Please say 'Hi' to Freddie for me. Bye."

"Elspeth, that was very rude, calling her at such a time..."

"It was a big golden retriever. His name was Goldie. Freddie named him. Mr. Clarke didn't have a place to bury Goldie after he killed him because their lawn is so small, and he didn't want the neighbors to see him digging a hole. He knew the house on the corner was empty, and so one night he took it there and buried it. That's what Patrick told me, too, so it must be true."

"All right, Elspeth, just go on to bed. We'll be up to tuck you in."

They *still* don't believe me, Elspeth thought, as she waited for her parents to come upstairs. What should I do now?

Chapter 28
Finding Hope in a Newfound Friend

The shelter wasn't very busy on Monday afternoon, and her dad held the door open while Elspeth all but ran in past him. There was a strong smell of the stuff they cleaned the floor with. Cages, each with a glass wall facing the viewing area, revealed at least two dozen cats of all ages, colors and sizes, some prowling, some meowing at passersby, others quietly curled into little balls, somehow managing to sleep through the ruckus. Elspeth wished she could take them all home, but...

"The dogs are through here," said a staff person who was dressed in blue hospital gloves and a white veterinarian's gown, holding a door open for Elspeth and her father that led into a long corridor lined with windowed compartments on both sides. A cacophony of barks and cries from up and down the hallway was almost deafening as prospective adopters filed past.

Elspeth had come in for a puppy, but she fell in love with every dog she saw. Older dogs with graying muzzles walked up to the glass, leaving wet nose prints, begging for freedom and a new family with their soulful brown eyes. A couple of them were plainly showing ribs, having probably been half-starved before the shelter took them in. One of the dogs, an older golden retriever, did not get up to greet them, nor even try to, his muzzle resting on his crossed forepaws, his eyebrows alternately raised and lowered as he passively watched the activity in the hallway from his corner. Elspeth stopped at the window of this dog and stared at him.

"Hey, Little Squirrel," Dad said, having walked past her a ways. "There are two down here that you might like."

"I'll be there in a minute..."

Dad walked back to her and looked at the graying animal. "Oh, but...that dog must be..."

"He's eight or eight-and-a-half, as far as we can tell," said the technician. "He was abandoned by the road and some nice people rescued him, brought him here. We call him Chester. He was neutered and had all his shots, and he's up to date on flea and tick treatments...just needs a lot of attention and TLC."

"Chester?" Elspeth asked.

"That's the name we gave him, and he answers to it. You could change it, of course, but I think he's been called Chester for so long it would be hard to call him something else now. He's been with us for almost three years. We're a no-kill shelter."

Dad said, "But aren't dogs this age...well, they're pretty susceptible to that disease...what is it...in their hips..."

"Dysplasia. Yes, of course, older dogs are harder for us to move out of here because of that. People don't want to get attached to older animals..."

"Memento mori," Elspeth said, quietly.

"...which is why we don't even have an adoption fee for him. He's a very sweet dog, and someone could make him feel very happy by getting him out of here."

"Honey, come on...there is a nice younger dog a few windows down, and a..."

"I want this one," she said.

Dad asked the technician, "Does he get along with other animals?"

"Oh, he's so mellow he'd probably mix well with any other dog, or cat."

"That's the one I want. And if he dies, he'll just come back as a ghost, like Goldie."

Almost as though Chester understood what she had said, he hobbled up to his feet and slowly approached the window, tail wagging.

"Hmm," the man in white said, "I've never seen him do that before...I think he loves you already, young lady. Would you like to take him for a walk? Right outside here?"

Elspeth clapped her hands excitedly. "Yes, please!"

"Well, I'll take you back to the waiting area for a few minutes, and then bring him out on a leash for you."

While seated in the waiting area, Dad noticed that Elspeth was smiling so widely that the dimple on her right cheek looked as deep as a puncture wound. He put his arm around her and smiled back at her. "What are you thinking, Little Squirrel?"

"About how I hope Chester likes me." She needn't have worried. When the dog was brought out on its leash on the opposite end of the long lobby, he looked around, spotted Elspeth among three or four other people, and pulled the technician right along toward her. He instantly began licking her hand. "Wow, Dad! He really does!"

She walked Chester – who behaved like a perfect gentleman by staying right at her side, seeming to know she was a bit hobbled – out the door and onto a wide grassy area. Dad grabbed a poop bag from an outdoor dispenser and carried it with him. The dog and Elspeth bonded immediately, destined to be inseparable.

But Dad and Elspeth had to leave the dog with the shelter, arranging to return for him in a week, after the house was made more dog-friendly. So, *next* Monday after school, Elspeth and Mom would pick her up and bring her to the shelter. Chester was very upset to see Elspeth walking toward the door without him, and he whined and pulled on his leash. Elspeth tried to ignore it, but it made her all the more anxious to have to wait seven more whole days before she could bring him home. She would stay busy getting everything ready for the new member of their family.

They stopped at a pet store on the way home and bought food and water bowls, a large, stuffed dog bed, a bunch of chew toys, a box of dog biscuits, a leash, collar, and a bag of dry food, which is what the attendant at the shelter had told them he'd been fed. Eventually they would need to go to City Hall to get a license, but only after they were confident they could keep him. Elspeth put the dog bed in her room, and right away began making a big banner from taped-together pieces of school writing paper, and using colored markers to write "Welcome Home, Chester!" across it.

Life was certainly looking up.

"Daddy, is it okay for me to walk him once a week down to the Clarkes' house so that Freddie can play with him?"

"That is something you will have to talk to Mrs. Clarke about. And I really don't want you walking that far..."

"It's just a few houses past the school. But Chester is the same kind of dog that Damon's and Freddie's was, and I want to share him...so that Freddie can have the same much. Or, at least, *some* of the same much."

"Some of the *what?*"

"Mom, is there any avocado for the salad tonight? Just lettuce and tomatoes and cucumbers is boring."

"Take one out of the vegetable drawer, sweetie," Mom said. "Do you know how to tell if it's ripe? Or how to cut it open?"

"No."

Her mom gave her a tutorial. Elspeth thought the huge pit inside was funny. "It takes up so much space in there!"

"You can actually grow an avocado plant with it. Keep it to the side and I'll show you how later."

Elspeth was wired, feeling tighter than a stretched rubber band. She didn't sleep well that night, but this time it was because she was brimming with joy about bringing home a new pet. This was going to be like early Christmas! At about two, she heard scratching at her bedroom door and thought: Oh, no...I forgot to leave it open for Lucie. She leaned over her bed and pulled the old crutch out, then hopped to the door, guided only by the new bulb in her night light. "Sorry, Lucie...I've never done *that* before..."

Lucie did not pass through the door when Elspeth opened it.

"Wait..."

She stuck her head through the door and looked both ways along the nearly pitch-dark hallway, listening for any sound.

There was motion in the air near her leg. Something brushed against her, and she pulled away, startled.

"Lucie?"

If this was the phantom dog, she wasn't really scared of it anymore, now believing it to be the ghost of Damon's golden retriever. But, what if it *wasn't* Damon's dog? If Goldie could be a ghost dog, so could a bad dog be, right?

She needed to turn on the light, as apprehensive as she was of doing so. "I'm turning on the light now...if you're Goldie, don't worry...you can stay."

She flicked on the light, and for a moment, everything seemed to be in its proper place. Then, a glance at her throw rug caused her to step backwards against the wall, and slide down to the floor, almost in a faint. Something shiny had been left on the rug. Something she had seen before.

"Nikki, Patrick...I wish you were here to see this..."

Chapter 29

The House on Bax and Beechum Streets

Elspeth made two quick phone calls as soon as she came downstairs on Tuesday morning. Hurrying through breakfast, she slopped milk and cereal on her place mat, and some of it splattered on the linoleum floor, which made Lucie profoundly happy. "I gotta go," she announced.

"You *have* to go," Mom reminded her.

"Mom!" she said, grinning.

"And where do you think you're going? The school bus will be here in less than a half-hour."

But Elspeth was already out the door.

Patrick, riding his bike, met her a few minutes later in front of Nikki's house. "What's the big emergency?" Nikki threw open her front door and ran to join them.

"Guys, this is so awesome!" Elspeth said, reaching into her pocket and holding out her palm. "I couldn't wait until school to show you this. It was on the floor in my bedroom last night."

Her friends gasped. "I want to go back to the house. We'll have to wait until Saturday morning, so it doesn't get dark while we're in there."

"I'm in," Patrick said. "We'll meet at the gate. We can talk about it more at school."

"I'll go with you guys," Nikki offered. "As far as

the gate."

"And then I get my new dog Monday after that. We're getting the house ready."

"Why do you need to get it ready, 'Speth?"

"Because we don't know if he'll chew things when he comes home, like wires and stuff. Probably not, because he's not a puppy, but just in case."

"The bus is coming pretty soon," Nikki reminded her friends.

"Yeah, I gotta go. See you in school, guys," Patrick said.

Elspeth was going back into the house after all.

The weather that week was bright and seasonally cool. Squirrels were grabbing up acorns for the winter and running to their nests. Most of the summer birds were gone, leaving crows, chickadees, and a few sparrows. The town looked different now, storefronts and churches and municipal buildings were colorless and forlorn, reluctantly bracing for the colder months. Snow was not yet in the forecast, but that could change overnight.

School days seemed to drag out longer than ever, so anxious was Elspeth to get back into the old house, and to pick up her dog. At recess, Elspeth, Nikki and Patrick walked back and forth across the macadam, where kids were shooting baskets from behind a line or doing layups. Others were skipping rope, and a few were chalking out hopscotch squares. "Are you nervous about going back to the house?" Nikki asked her friends.

"I ain't," Patrick said.

"Not anymore," Elspeth answered. "I know what's

in there."

"Well, what *is* in there?" asked Nikki.

"I talked to Mrs. Clarke on the phone, and she told me what Patrick told me at school – that Damon's dad buried their dog under the lawn of that house. So, it must be true, right? It's walking around in there. It's been trying to make friends with me. It comes to my house. It's so lonely..."

"But, you're saying you want to be friends with a *dead dog*!"

Elspeth said, "Forget it, Nik." Then she asked, "Are you guys ever worried about dying?"

"What d'ya mean?" Patrick asked.

"Well, I dunno. Do you ever think about some day when you have to die?"

"Yeah, but not very much," Nikki said. "Once in a while. I mean, like, why worry a lot about it if it's gonna happen anyway, right?"

Patrick seemed confused about her question. "Why would you ask that? *Everything* dies. Trees die, animals die, fish die. We die. So?"

"It doesn't bother you?"

"What if it did? How would that change anything? Right?"

After a few moments of quiet between the friends, Elspeth repeated, "I can't wait until Saturday."

Of course, Elspeth had to wait, but Saturday morning did finally arrive, and it was time to meet her friends on their latest venture to the corner house. She and Nikki had just rounded the corner onto Bax Street, when Patrick came into view. "Hey, guys. You ready?"

Nikki stopped at the corner, and pointed with her arm held out straight as a broom handle. "Look! There!"

Elspeth and Patrick followed her gaze. "What?"

"There! Well, now you *missed* it!"

"Missed what, Nik?"

"*A window shade just got pulled up!* They were all down a minute ago, and then that one went up!" There was now a solitary window on the second floor that was unblocked by a shade or curtains.

"Wish I could see in," Elspeth said.

"I'm more worried about what's looking *out*. At *us*."

"Well, we can find out right now, Nik," Elspeth said, leading the way around the corner of the building to see if the side door might be open from Halloween night, when she and Nikki and Damon had escaped the building. No luck – it was shut and locked tight. "I really wish you hadn't closed the door behind you when you ran out that night."

Patrick offered to go back to the broken window in front, and come to the door from the inside to open it for the girls. "You guys can just wait here. No sweat." He then ran around the corner to the porch, while the girls stayed put.

Nikki, who had once again relented and come to the house with her friends, quite reasonably asked, "And *why* are we going in there again?"

"To see what pulled that window shade open. And to try to convince Goldie to leave this place, and maybe go stay with Freddie. And, thanks for coming with us, Nik. You're really pretty brave after all, you know that?"

Nikki smiled warmly, but then asked, "Goldie?"

"Damon's dog. That was his name. And, because he's a ghost dog, I'm pretty sure this is where he'd live. Right?"

"*Pretty* sure? Jeez, 'Speth..."

"Just kidding, Nik. I'm really, *really* sure that's him in there."

"But not Damon?"

"I don't know where Damon is buried, but it wasn't here. He's in a cemetery some place. But maybe he visits here now, to be with his dog."

Getting through the window was more easily achieved this time, mostly because Patrick could see what he was doing. Once the girls had been let inside, they were stunned by the intensity of the color. The door and stairs and floor were flooded with red light from the sun pouring through the stain glass windows. "This is like that old lady's house on Halloween!" Nikki observed. "And like our tent with my red light on."

Elspeth said, "Too much. They should have used different colored glass when they built this, not just red." Then she called, "Goldie! Com'ere, boy!" At the bottom of the stairway, Elspeth asked her friends, "Okay...you guys going up with me?" Nobody objected, so Elspeth grabbed the railing and cautiously climbed with Patrick right behind her in case she stumbled. Every step creaked as they put their feet down.

Daytime or not, it was still sunless and quite dim on the second floor, and the three frequently squinted to better see into the rooms. There were four large bedrooms and one smaller one, a few closets, and a bathroom that had a clawfoot bathtub, which was held slightly aloft by four short legs with feet about the size of big dog paws. The girls giggled when they saw these. "Not fair...an old bathtub gets four legs, and I only have *one*!"

"Can you imagine it walking away while you were taking a bath?" Nikki joked, nervously trying to lighten the creepy mood. "Wouldn't it be embarrassing...you only have soap bubbles covering you and the tub just leaves the bathroom and goes out the door and wanders down Beechum Street? I mean, you can't just get out of it in the middle of Siteson, right?"

Elspeth was able to form a mental impression of what this house might have looked like when it was still lived in and kept up. In her imagination, faded wallpaper became crisp and colorful; the stairs were suddenly newly-carpeted and the banister polished. There would have been a lot of old but beautifully restored furniture, such as antique dressers and desks and love seats. The place would have smelled slightly rustic from the pine wood floors, but clean, and there would have been no cobwebs or mouse droppings in sight. Upstairs, where she now stood, a large family once slept at night, in a master bedroom for the parents, and the rest for what might well have been a sizable brood of children.

Somehow, though, she could not imagine a dog living here, without any companionship.

But there *was* a dog in the house, because all three kids had heard it.

They walked into each of the bedrooms, calling for Goldie. Cracked and yellowed window shades had been drawn, and dusty curtains pulled together. In none of them were there any mirrors, picture frames, throw rugs or furniture of any kind.

Except in one room, the last they came to. It contained an old, brass bed frame, a moth-eaten mattress, and two pillows with no cases, revealing holes from which goose feathers stuck out. Covering the bed were a few tussled blankets.

Nikki and Elspeth wandered inside, and Nikki said, "*This* is the room? The window shade's up! You think Damon stays here? *Is he in the room with us right now?*"

"Damon?" Elspeth called, several times. "Goldie?"

"I think we should get out of here," Nikki said. "*Please*!"

"Are you here, Damon?"

"Come on, 'Speth, it's really dangerous for us to be here..."

"What, you think that if Damon lives here he's going to hurt us?"

"There's a staircase going to the third floor...maybe to an attic," Patrick said from the hallway, then joining them in the room. "Want to check it out?"

"Not me!" Nikki shouted, predictably.

"I don't think we need to, Patrick, he wouldn't be up there." Using a steady, nurturing voice, Elspeth continued calling, "Goldie...remember me? If you're in here somewhere, I want to thank you for visiting me at my home. And if Damon is with you..."

The growl of a large animal, echoing a little through empty rooms and up the stairwell from somewhere on the ground floor, sent a wave of apprehension through Elspeth, followed by the certainty that Goldie was answering her call. She moved into the hall to greet him, and the others followed.

Then, it appeared.

At the bottom of the staircase stood a dog. A real, live, visible animal the size of a mastiff but the shape of a Great Dane, with brown and black stripes on its coat, polar bear-size paws, and lethal teeth from a young child's worst nightmare.

The creature began to slowly lope up the steps toward the children, cutting off any escape route, growling all the way. Patrick and the girls ran into the room with the bed and shut the door behind them. Nikki screamed when she felt the hot breath of something against her leg. "Get away from me!"

But then, from the *other* side of the door, they could still hear the huge dog snarling. It began to scratch the wood, but then banged into it, presumably with its head. Thump. Thump.

"If that thing is out *there*, what the hell is in *here*?" Patrick cried.

From way downstairs, a voice shouted, "*Elspeth!*"

"It's Daddy!" Elspeth said. "*We're up here! Upstairs!*" she called, near to shrieking.

Patrick felt a pocket of warm air weaving through his legs, and jumped back.

"Can we climb out through a window?" Nikki screamed, desperately.

"Too high!" said Patrick.

"And *I* couldn't do it with my fake leg!"

The growling from the hall intensified. They could hear Mr. Amesbury moving quickly up the stairs. "Elspeth?" Then they heard "Oof!" and what sounded like a person tumbling down steps to the bottom. Wanting to help him, Elspeth heedlessly threw open the bedroom door and, rounding the hallway corner, looked down the staircase, where she saw her dad lying on the bottom step, his legs stretched out across the foyer floor.

"*Daddy*!" The dog was standing over him, saliva oozing from its black, rubbery lips. Its head turned and looked up in Elspeth's direction, then walked over her motionless father and began a second ascent up the stairs. The children were now sandwiched between a dog they could see and something behind them they couldn't. They began running in uncoordinated directions, panicking, not knowing where they would be safe.

All three wound up in the bathroom, with Patrick backed against the door to keep it blocked. Elspeth and Nikki climbed into the clawfoot bathtub and clung tightly to one another. They heard the dog padding along in the hall, sniffing, looking for them. At one moment they were sure its nose was right at the bottom of the bathroom door, but then it moved away.

Mr. Amesbury had apparently been knocked out cold from his fall, for he made not a sound. The children did not speak, for fear of being overheard.

BOOM! Patrick felt a powerful judder as the dog on the other side rammed into the door again and again. BOOM! BOOM! The muscles in the boy's legs and arms and hands strained to hold back the attack, but the door bolt suddenly splintered and exploded inward, sending a metal plate and some screws scattering at his feet, while pushing Patrick forward.

A mammoth, snarling snout poked through and was trying to further push the door open, its yellowed teeth bared.

Elspeth, believing now she'd been wrong all along, squeezed her eyes shut with the belief that she and Nikki and Patrick, like Damon, were about to die while only ten years old. But, she heard a groan from her father downstairs, and thought: Daddy...Daddy could die, too.

The noise from the hallway stopped.

Patrick was able to push the door closed, but again had to throw his weight against it. There was no sound of paws walking the floor. No growling. Elspeth thought: it's going back down for Daddy...

She climbed out of the tub and went to the door. "Out of the way, Patrick..."

"Uh-uh. That thing is still out there. *Right outside the door.*"

"We have to save Daddy. Please. I don't think it's right at the door now."

"*No*, Elspeth!"

But, after a full minute of hearing nothing, Patrick cautiously stepped away from the door and let it open narrowly. He pulled it open further and poked his head through, looking out to both sides of the hallway. "Okay, let's see if we can get out of here..."

Elspeth pulled Nikki from the tub, and the three traumatized friends moved incrementally into the hallway. When they reached the top of the stairs, Elspeth saw that her father was still at the bottom, his position unchanged. There was no animal in sight. "Oh, Daddy!" she said, and grabbed the railing to go to the bottom, but stopped when she heard Nikki scream.

Her friend had been knocked to the floor with a thud. The wind was forced out of her as she felt pressure on her diaphragm, and hot breath blew into her face, her nose and lungs filling with a foul odor like that of sour milk. The dog's head was so huge, it blocked everything else in the hallway from Nikki's view. A repulsive blob of dark, matted fur with a sharp snout and homicidal eyes, it was now only inches away from her face. The massive brute drooled on her chin and cheek, and into her mouth. Spitting out the vile-tasting droplets, and trying her best not to gag, she cried, "*Help me! Patrick! Elspeth!*"

Patrick was momentarily frozen in place with shock, but Elspeth deliberately fell backwards on her butt right beside the struggling Nikki, who was waving her hands in front of her face to ward off her attacker. She yanked down her lining and quickly removed her prosthesis. Holding it by the upper leg with both hands, she began swinging the foot in the direction of the dog, which was close enough to her so that she could land a few good hits to its rump. "*Get away from her!*" The animal yelped and turned toward her, moving off Nikki's chest.

Elspeth called, "*Daddy!*" Her father was now conscious and pulling his way up the railing, unable to move quickly because his fall had injured him.

"Elspeth!" Her father had made it halfway up the stairs. "*Elspeth!*"

But his daughter, still sitting on the hallway floor, was now staring directly into the bloodshot eyes of this demon dog, while Patrick and Nikki scrambled to find a way to help her. "*Elspeth!*" Elspeth took another hard swing with her prosthesis and hit the dog firmly on its muzzle, causing it to shake its head furiously and wail like a wounded banshee.

"Here, Daddy! Right at the top of the stairs!"

Just before the dog could sink its teeth into Elspeth's arm, it began twisting itself this way and that in a crazy blur, apparently trying to bite at something the kids couldn't see. It cried out in pain and retreated briefly into one of the rooms. "Daddy!"

"I'm...I'm...okay..." he answered, trying to catch his breath.

Elspeth grabbed the railing, Patrick picked up the leg she'd left behind, and the three made their way down the stairs. Mr. Amesbury turned to go down just ahead of them. But, as quickly as they could descend the stairs, they heard the paws of the unseen creature, which was already downstairs with them. There followed a tremendous yowl that filled the house, coming from the top of the stairs. The sound was guttural and evil, from a dog that clearly wanted a victim, wanted to kill. It was coming directly down toward Elspeth and her father. The bottom of the stairs was bathed in red from the stained glass windows, so everything looked like an inferno.

Patrick and Nikki backed against the wall, unable to move, as the dog passed them by.

"Help us!" Elspeth implored. "Hit it with my leg!"

Patrick cautiously moved toward the enormous dog, which was occupied with Elspeth and her father, and lifted the leg above his shoulder, sending its foot directly into the animal's back. Nikki, meanwhile, tried to kick it, but missed, because the creature was moving too fast. Then, the creature's snarling inexplicably became a series of howls and whimpers and the chaotic clicking of long toenails moving backward and forward and around in small circles.

The kids could see fur from the dog's back being pulled up and ripped out, tufts of it left to float down to the floor. There was a pained "yip," followed by the grizzled, agonized cries of a wounded animal as it fell several times, snapping its jaws at the air, trying to defend itself against an unseen force. Yet, not quite unseen...an indefinable, translucent shape was coming at the dog, over and over again. Then the foyer went quiet as the big dog vanished deep into the house, crying and limping.

Patrick and Nikki, nearly in shock, raced to Elspeth, who was kneeling on the floor beside her father, massaging his back as he got to his hands and knees. She asked him time and time again if he was badly hurt. "No, Little Squirrel," he assured her. "I'm...I'll...be all right. Can you... Patrick, can you and Nikki help me up?"

Elspeth took her prosthetic from Patrick, returning it to its sleeve, and she and Mr. Amesbury were brought to their feet. There was blood on the floor, which looked black in the red light, all smeared near to where they stood, but trailing off in small, round spots that eventually disappeared down the hall and around a corner.

Mr. Amesbury hadn't been badly wounded and had not been bitten. Maybe a slight concussion. As he was being helped to his feet, legs shaking, he saw something. He couldn't be certain what it was. There seemed to be an indistinct outline moving back and forth to his side in the crimson light, in the nebulous shape of...a dog? Goldie? He decided that his daughter may have been right. The moment Patrick opened the side door and let natural light through, the shape disappeared, and the four traumatized housebreakers stumbled out and onto the lawn.

Chapter 30
The Old Lady, and the Way Back to Normal

Elspeth, Nikki, Patrick and Mr. Amesbury sat out on the side lawn of the old house, exhausted and panting. "Dad...I'm so glad you came here, but how did you know where I went?"

"I can't explain it, really. I was changing from my church clothes and you had already left to meet your friends and...I felt a nudge on my elbow. At first, I thought I'd touched something in the room. But I was in the middle of the room, and there was nothing..."

Elspeth squeezed her father's arm and pressed her face against it. "Was it a dog?"

"I...can't make sense of it. Logic told me, 'This can't be happening,' but obviously, it was. And at that moment I knew that you had gone back to the house. I felt you were in danger. Maybe you three can help me with this part: if this is your ghost dog, don't ghosts have rules? If you can't see it, how can you feel it touching you? If it leaves tracks in the dew outside, why isn't the dog itself visible? Aren't there rules for ghosts? I think I may have seen what saved us from that horrible creature that attacked us. I know you all helped me, but something else..."

"Yeah, there *was* something else," Nikki said.

"Goldie," Elspeth said, with absolute assurance. "We need to go back to that old lady's house. Daddy, you need to buy the skull from her."

"What skull?"

"I think there are *two* dogs living in this house, and they don't get along very well. One is Damon's dog, Goldie, the one who saved us, but the one you can't see. That's his skull. The other dog...the dangerous one that tried to kill us, is...I don't know...a wild stray dog, probably. Not sure. Maybe if we buy Goldie's skull from the lady and bury it on the property of the house where it belongs...I mean, the rest of its skeleton must be under the ground somewhere on this lawn. Maybe right underneath where we're sitting."

"And how do you figure that would make a difference?" her father asked.

"Maybe if the whole skeleton is all in one place, or at least under one lawn, Goldie can stop haunting this house, and find a better place to stay, away from that scary dog."

"Oh, come on, 'Speth, that's stupid," Nikki said.

"Is it stupider than anything else that's happened?" Elspeth demanded. "I'm just guessing. Worth a try though, isn't it? Daddy?"

"Who is the lady with the skull?"

"I dunno. We don't remember her from trick-or-treating last year. Maybe she just moved here."

"She might be a witch," Nikki suggested. "I mean, she had her house all lit with a red light, and..."

"Oh, Nikki! When has anyone ever *seen* Goldie?"

"Never," Nikki said.

"No, *you* saw him. When you turned the red part of your flashlight on...you know, when we camped out, you saw something moving, right? When we were at the old lady's house, which was all red inside, I saw something. And I saw it again in Mom's and Dad's room because the light from their clock is red. I couldn't see it in my bedroom because my clock has green numbers. And, Daddy, you said you just saw something in the house a few minutes ago, because the light through the windows was red! There's something about that color..."

The four of them thought that over for a time, and no one could offer an explanation.

"Please, Daddy? Just ask the lady if she would sell that skull. Okay? Please? You can keep my allowance until it's paid back."

Mr. Amesbury was still a bit short of breath, and looked at the children's faces, one after the other. They were all pleading with their eyes for him to be their hero now, and decided he absolutely owed it to Elspeth to do this small favor for her, even if her theory didn't really make sense. "Take me to the old lady's house, and I'll have a word with her," he said. He felt an extra squeeze on his arm from his daughter, and the four of them stood up and walked to the old iron gate, where Mr. Amesbury's car was parked.

"I'm just really happy that you're all right, Little Squirrel."

"Daddy!" she scolded, but then added, "I'm glad you are, too. I'm *really* glad you weren't at work or somewhere."

Patrick snickered. "Little *Squirrel*?"

Nikki said, "Shut up, Patrick."

From the windows of her father's car, Elspeth and her friends tried to navigate their way back to the house where the old lady lived. It had not been well-lit that Halloween night, and they weren't sure which house it was as they passed along Bax Street opposite the school. "Look...in the bushes." High in the shrubbery, in front of a modest, gray-shingled house, hung a tissue ghost that had been one of many on Halloween night. "She must have missed one. This is the house. I'm sure of it."

The door was answered by a graying woman who had kind and welcoming eyes. "Hello. What can I do for you all?" Of course, she looked nothing like who the kids had seen on Halloween night. She'd been hunched over like a feeble crone then, now she stood straight and much taller. Her foyer was brightly-lit, and no animal skull rested on her table.

Elspeth's father said, "Hello, ma'am. I'm Ray Amesbury. My daughter Elspeth and her friends," he went on, holding his daughter's shoulders, "came by your house on Halloween and were shown the skull of a..."

"A dog...yes, that's right. I used it to give the trick-or-treaters a thrill."

"Do you *know* that it's from a dog?"

"Oh, yes...the shape is unmistakable. I found that on the property of the old house..."

"That's what the kids told me."

Patrick interjected, "Not me...I wasn't with them on Halloween."

"Would you all like to come in?"

"Just for a few minutes, thank you," Elspeth's father said.

Nikki asked, "Was there just a skull, or a whole skeleton?"

"The skull is all I found. I looked around for more, but..."

Elspeth was checking out the woman's house. There were cheery yellow flowers on the wallpaper. She could see the keyboard of a piano through the doorway into an adjacent parlor. Pictures on her hallway walls depicted the woman, maybe thirty years younger then, with a tall man and two older children, all smiling widely. This was a friendly place, after all. "Ma'am...would you let us buy that skull?"

The woman looked down at Elspeth, puzzled. "What on earth for, dear?"

Before she could answer, her father said, "Oh, my daughter has decided that..." He checked himself momentarily, realizing how absurd he was going to sound. "She believes that there is a dog spirit living in that house, and that if its skull is returned to the property, it might...I know this may seem a little bizarre...it might stop haunting the house."

The woman looked at the hopeful faces of the children. "Hmm. Well, sweeties, I am not anchored to that skull, and I'll give it to you. No charge. Would that work for you?"

Elspeth wrapped her arms around the woman's waist and thanked her several times. Nikki noticed that a tear ran down the woman's face, as she returned the hug.

Using his hands and a sturdy stick, Mr. Amesbury dug the hole into which the skull was to be buried. This was a bit difficult, as the ground was no longer soft. "What I really need is a trowel. Obviously, I wish you hadn't gone into the house in the first place, but it's done now."

Nikki asked, "Are you gonna tell my parents that

we broke into the house?"

"Hmm. Good question. I should, you know."

Still shaking, and a bit contrite, Nikki murmured, "Yes, sir...I know."

"Of course, I broke into it also. I'll leave that to you. My advice is to tell them, so they don't hear it from someone else first. Same with you, Patrick."

"My mom doesn't care, but I'll tell her."

"But you could probably leave out the ghost dog part. Meanwhile, I will definitely have animal control take care of the...the dog we all *saw* in there so it won't harm anyone else." Mr. Amesbury finished filling the dirt in over the skull, and patting down the sod, while the kids knelt around him. He leaned back and looked at his daughter. "As for the invisible animal...I don't know. I'm not sure how to talk about that with anyone, or even what it really is, or what I should do about it..."

"You don't have to do anything, Daddy. It's Goldie. He's friendly. He was the one who came into our house those nights, and he didn't hurt anybody. He's probably with us right now, watching over us."

Patrick said, "He is. I know he is. And I want him to follow me home and go to the Clarkes' house. It would be cool if he stayed there with Freddie, to protect him in case his dad gets mean again. He sure protected us today. Wish I could pat him."

"Maybe you can," Elspeth said. "I haven't tried to yet."

"I really can't explain all this to the police, even to Detective Todd, so I don't think I'll try," Mr. Amesbury said. "A month ago I thought ghosts were just for Halloween and movies and horror stories. I think you have to actually meet up with one to believe in them. But we're all okay, and that's what matters."

Elspeth was happy, and very proud of her dad. It was like they had just bonded with each other all over again. That mattered, too.

Chapter 31
Theories

School lunch was a bevy of excitement as Patrick, Elspeth and Nikki breathlessly shared their story with the rest of the boys at one of the back tables. Nobody even picked up a fork as they listened, mesmerized.

Elspeth was in charge of recounting the story as best she could, trying to remember every small detail...except, of course, the one part about Freddie. Patrick and Nikki filled in small gaps here and there.

"Jeez," one of the wide-eyed boys said, "you guys really think there's a ghost? For *real*?"

Another said, "Well, that fake leg of yours really came in handy, huh?"

"Yeah, but there's more. Look at this," Elspeth said, pulling a small shiny object from her pocket and putting it on the table between them. "I think the last time something came into my house, it wasn't Damon' dog. I think it was *Damon's ghost.*" The kids all stared at the center of the table as though a twenty-pound ice cream sundae had suddenly appeared there.

"He was wearing that when he was buried," Patrick said of the gold-colored ring, engraved with the letters 'D.C.'. "I know because his mom said she wanted to take it off his finger so that she could keep it at her home, but she didn't think to at the time 'cause she was too upset."

Elspeth felt her eyes watering, as they did every time she looked at the ring. "God, I miss him." Then, shaking her head to stabilize her feelings, she explained, "A few nights ago, I felt something come into my room, and when I turned on the light, I saw that ring on my rug. Then, I said hello to Damon out loud, but no one answered. So I said, 'If you're Damon, you should tell Goldie to go keep Freddie company, because I'm getting a new dog, and Freddie needs him more than I do.' I don't know if he will go there and visit Freddie or not. I'm not sure why the dog kept coming to me instead of to the Clarkes' house. Or why he didn't visit you, Patrick...or you, Nikki."

"Well," Patrick said, "actually, Goldie *has* visited me. And I think Damon has, too, and that's why I believed you when you first told me about the dog in your bedroom. That's why I wasn't scared of going into the house. 'Course, I didn't know there was a *live* dog in there, too."

Nikki felt left out. "Why didn't he visit *me*?"

"Dunno. Maybe you just aren't...aren't the kind of person who can sense a ghost when it's around," Elspeth said, patting her friend on the back. "I'll bet you *were* visited...you just didn't know you were."

"It's okay. I really don't want no ghosts in my house, anyway."

"You know," Patrick suggested, "I really don't think any of us should share what happened yesterday with anyone else. *We* all believe it because we knew Damon, and I knew Goldie, too. And everything that happened in the house on Saturday...even Elspeth's father believes now. But no one else would. So, when we talk about it, let's only do it here or on the playground, okay?"

The others agreed. As Elspeth slipped the ring back into her pocket, she declared, "I'm going to give this to Mrs. Clarke." Changing the subject to something more upbeat, she said, "Mom's picking me up right after school, and I'm going to get my new dog Chester. Maybe once a week I'll walk him to the Clarkes' so that Freddie can play with him. Mom and Dad said I could as long as someone is with me."

"I'll go!" volunteered one of the boys whose name Elspeth did not know yet. It was then she knew she was making new friends, even aside from Chester.

"Anyway, none of us has eaten lunch and it's almost time to bring our trays up."

The lunch ladies eyed the kids from the back table as they brought their nearly-full trays up to the garbage can.

"Wait a minute, people," one of the women said. "Just what is this, a hunger strike?"

"Nah," Patrick said. "Just grody food."

The woman squinted her eyes to narrow slits and frowned. "Well, I'm going to be here all week, and I'd better not see this happen again. Bring your own lunches instead of wasting ours."

"Yes, ma'am."

The kids giggled as they rounded the corner into the hallway and dispersed to their various classrooms. At the end of the school day, Elspeth picked up her backpack, said goodbye to Mrs. Ewell, and departed to meet her mother at the curb.

Chapter 32
Coda

Elspeth's mom drove her to the shelter to pick Chester up after school. He had been freshly-groomed and had a lustrous, gold-orange coat. "Such a pretty boy," Mom said to the dog, patting his head. She was sure that Chester smiled at her before eagerly jumping into the car, as though he'd ridden in it for years. On the way home, Elspeth ran his thick, feathery tail through her hands, even as she was being covered with grateful canine kisses.

Once home, Lucie hissed at Chester and backed away with flattened ears, but after a few days, the two were even playing with one another. Each night, the dog deeply sniffed Elspeth's throw rug as though he'd detected the scent of another dog, before circling around it about five times and finally settling down for the night. He completely ignored the fluffy dog bed that had been brought home for him, although Lucie used it in the daytime. Rather than always sleeping on Elspeth's bed, Lucie sometimes chose to curl up against Chester until their breathing was synchronized and both fell comfortably to sleep.

Goldie's ghost never returned to further haunt Elspeth, who began sleeping very soundly, waking ready for every new day with renewed kid energy.

So that Freddie could play with him, Elspeth made

good on her promise to walk Chester all the way to the Clarkes' house with Nikki for a visit. Mrs. Clarke was so grateful for the offer that she smiled. It was the first time Elspeth had seen that happen. "You know, Freddie's been acting strangely the past few weeks. He's been talking to someone a lot...well, an imaginary friend, I guess, and calling it 'Goldie.' Of course, that was the name of our dog..."

The girls looked at each other, and grinned. Elspeth said, "You probably won't need for us to bring Chester, then. But can we please still visit Freddie sometimes?"

"Oh, he would love that. I had to quit my job and apply for a food card to be with him more, so we'll both be here and you can come by any time."

"Is it okay to just go say hello to him right now?" Elspeth asked, and Mrs. Clarke told them to go right to his bedroom. They could hear him laughing even before they reached the end of the hall. Little Freddie was rolling about on the floor, kicking his feet in the air. He giggle-shouted, "That tickles, Goldie!" Then he saw the girls and Chester, and waved, but went right back to his playing. Elspeth gave Freddie a hug from behind, and he hardly peered back at her. Chester began barking, looking not quite directly at Freddie, but to his sides, his gaze moving around the room as though following a housefly.

"Awesome," Nikki said.

"Yeah, you got *that* right." Elspeth pulled a small wrapped package from her pocket. "Here, Freddie, I brought you something..." The boy took this from her hand, curious. "It's a night light," she told him.

"I already have one," Freddie said.

"Not like this. This one's red, so you can see Goldie a little better when it's dark."

"Oh, okay! Thanks"

"Thank *you*, Goldie," Elspeth said, turning to leave. "C'mon Chester." Once back in the kitchen, they were offered cookies to take home. "Mrs. Clarke, Freddie's going to be fine. He really is," Elspeth assured her. Mrs. Clarke looked a bit puzzled, but returned their smile. She thanked the children over and over for bringing her Damon's ring. Elspeth had white-lied and told her Damon had given it to her at school. She was obviously very confused about that, as she swore Damon had been wearing it when he was closed into his casket.

As she had almost every year, Elspeth had to have measurements taken at the prosthetist's office.

"It'll be a week or two before your new leg is ready," the doctor said. "And what happened here?" he asked, indicating the somewhat bent toes of the prosthesis she was still using.

"Oh, I guess I stubbed it on something."

Mr. Clarke's murder charge was dropped just before Thanksgiving, based on a lack of evidence. Freddie's involvement on the tragic night never made it into the news, so most people still thought Mr. Clarke to be guilty, because he had earlier admitted to it. The police, of course, knew that was not the case. He had confessed in order to protect Freddie. During a TV interview from jail, he admitted to his drinking and violent behavior. After the murder charge against him was dropped, he still had to spend months behind bars for hurting his wife, but swore many times that he would stop drinking, attend AA, and be a better father and husband, which remained to be seen. He'd be on probation, which made it against the law for him to drink alcohol.

Elspeth received her new prosthetic leg the second week of December, and this time it looked like a real leg from knee to foot, with an outer plastic shell that was contoured to resemble the shape and appearance of actual skin with bone and muscle inside. She could wear a dress now, and leggings, and did so for Sunday School and, in May, for her eleventh birthday party.

Her party was, she thought, going to be on Saturday afternoon at two, so she didn't bother getting dressed for breakfast, and came downstairs in her pajamas. No one was there, no breakfast was being prepared. Chester and Lucie stood looking at her as though to say, "Well, are you going to feed us? It's that time."

"Mom? Dad? Hello!"

Then, she heard a giggle from somewhere in the house. "Chester, is there someone hiding around here? Go on, boy...go find 'em!"

Chester sat down, cocked his head, and looked at her with an expression of, "What are you trying to tell me?"

She looked in Daddy's office. She checked the basement. The garage. Behind all the furniture. For just a tiny moment, she started feeling worried. Almost as an afterthought, she opened the large walk-in closet in the hallway and heard a loud "pop!" followed by a burst of colored streamers falling from over her head. "Happy Birthday!" everyone inside the closet shouted, and out walked Mom, Dad, Nikki, Patrick, Mrs. Clarke and Freddie, who giggled again.

"You scared the you-know-what out of me!" Elspeth said, regaining her breath and pulling paper streamers from her shoulders and hair.

Freddie said, "We had to stay quiet for a long time...maybe a whole day!"

Elspeth changed into her dress and stockings and the seven of them drove in two cars to a nearby restaurant for a late breakfast. Back at home, she was presented with a vanilla cake in the shape of her old prosthetic leg. "That's *really* a weird idea," Elspeth said to her mom, who had baked it. But she thought it was pretty funny, which was the point. After all, it didn't *taste* like a plastic and metal leg...it tasted like cake.

Patrick gave her a gift-wrapped CD of a singer she really liked. Nikki gave her a catnip mouse for Lucie and a chew toy for Chester. Mrs. Clarke had made her a huge batch of chocolate chip cookies. Freddie said, "I got to eat some of those." Then he proudly handed her a box he had wrapped in a jumble of paper with tape completely covering it, which made it hard to open. "That's from me!" he boasted. Inside the box were five crayons, two of which were partly used. "I don't like those colors, so you can have them."

Elspeth squatted down to Freddie's level and gave him a hug. "Thanks, Freddie...that's a great present. Thanks *everybody*!"

Chester was walking in odd patterns around the living room, as though following something. He barked a few times and whined a little as the Clarkes left for home. "Come on, Goldie," Freddie said to empty space, before turning back to Elspeth and bragging, "I'm having pisgetti and beach balls for dinner!" Then, the Amesbury house went quiet. Chester commenced to sniff out the living room carpet, over and over again.

Dinner that night was Elspeth's favorite: leg of lamb with mashed potatoes and gravy, green beans, mint jelly, and garlic bread. But there was one other item on her plate when it was put in front of her: three creamed onions. "Mom!! You know I hate those! They make me sick."

Mom said, "Yes, but the rule here has always been, you have to try a little of everything, so eat at least one."

"But...it only takes *one* to make me puke!" Elspeth did not see Mom wink at her father. "So, you're gonna torture me on my birthday?" she asked, nearly gagging at the mere thought of putting a creamed onion into her mouth. Then she noticed her parents quietly laughing. "Oh, ha! You were just trying to fake me out." Elspeth started laughing. "But can you take them off my plate? I don't want them to rub against the other stuff." Then she said, "That was a really cool birthday. The best ever. Thanks for the surprise breakfast...how did you keep Freddie quiet while I was looking for you guys?"

"Wasn't easy, Miss Eleven-Year-Old, but it was fun," Dad said. "And we haven't given you every present yet. There's one more."

Elspeth's eyes grew wide. "What is it?"

"It's waiting for you in the driveway."

Elspeth moved faster on her new prosthetic leg

than she ever had out the door, where for a moment she looked around, seeing nothing but driveway and neighborhood. Then, there it was, sticking out just a little from the back side of the garage: a rear tire with a red reflector mounted above it. The bike was colored glittery pastel blue, had a bucket seat, a basket, handlebar streamers, a bell, training wheels, and a package of decals. Sitting atop the seat was a matching blue helmet with gold decals that spelled out her name. "As soon as you get used to using that with your new leg, we'll take off the training wheels."

"Oh, Daddy..." She really couldn't think of anything to say to express her joy.

So she cried. How could such a terrible autumn and winter have turned into such a wonderful spring?

The topics of Damon and the mystery dog – no longer a mystery, it seemed – did not often come up anymore at home or at school. Elspeth, Patrick and Nikki hung out after school and on weekends a lot. All three, and probably most of the rest of the fourth grade, were a bit anxious about having to change schools in the fall. The Siteson Middle School was further away from where they lived, and they would not be able to walk to or from it. Plus, there was the matter of suddenly being the youngest students instead of the oldest ones they'd been all year. New bullies would emerge and probably be more difficult than those they'd already dealt with. Maybe the teachers would be stricter, and they'd have to change classes every hour. In Elspeth's case, she knew she was going to miss Mrs. Ewell, who had been so kind.

The three friends had become an indivisible trio,

which Patrick named The Vagabonds. Elspeth even went with Patrick to a couple of matinees while Nikki, although she'd been invited and wanted to go, declined to join them. Trying very hard to tame her jealousy, she thought her friends should have time to themselves.

The temperaments of Elspeth's mom and dad seemed to have leveled out a lot after Elspeth adopted Chester and got her new leg, and they did not argue much anymore, except about the usual grown-up stuff like money and "Elspeth, you didn't change the litter box," and "Little Squirrel, why is there a C+ on your report card?" (It was because she hadn't studied for several history tests, which was unlike her).

So, life went on with these good, good friends, who had many adventures together.
    And, if you ever happen to move to the town of Siteson, and have to walk past the old house on your way home from school, slow down at the corner. Hear anything?
    But, then, walk on.
    Better to just leave alone what or whoever might now occupy the house in the town of Siteson on the corner of Bax and Beechum Streets.

THE END

www.ingramcontent.com/pod-product-compliance
Lightning Source LLC
Chambersburg PA
CBHW021405290426
44108CB00010B/396